Pi Math Contest Volume 3
Middle School Contests 2019-2021

AlphaStar Academy
Math Development Team

© 2023 AlphaStar Academy. All rights reserved.

About Pi Math Contest

Pi Math Contest (PiMC) is an annual math competition organized by AlphaStar Academy. It has three divisions: Euler division for elementary school students, Fermat division for middle school students, and Gauss division for high school students. PiMC started in 2015 for elementary school students. In 2019 and 2023, it expanded to include middle school and high school students, respectively.

The primary goals of the contest are to stimulate interest and achievement in mathematics and to provide recognition of outstanding young mathematicians, their dedicated teachers, and schools.

PiMC is written by a team of AlphaStar Academy teachers and alumni.

About AlphaStar Academy

AlphaStar Academy is an education company based in California. It offers extensive training programs for gifted students towards national and international Math and Science competitions such as American Mathematics Competitions, MATHCOUNTS, USA Math Olympiads, USA Computing Olympiads, and F=ma.

Students and teams from AlphaStar Academy performed extremely well in Mathematics competitions and Olympiads, with countless students finishing in the top 10 and teams finishing in first place in competitions including Harvard-MIT Math Tournament, Princeton Math Competition, Stanford Math Tournament, Berkeley Math Tournament, and Caltech Harvey Mudd Math Competition. Over the past decade, more than 150 AlphaStar students got perfect scores in the American Mathematics Competitions (AMC 8/10/12), most of the MATHCOUNTS California team members were AlphaStar students, and more than a dozen AlphaStar students joined the USA team for the International Math Olympiads.

Starting 2020, AlphaStar Academy has started offering all of its courses and programs online:

https://alphastar.academy/

Acknowledgements

These tests were written by AlphaStar faculty and alumni who have participated and got excellent results in Math competitions and Olympiads. We thank everyone involved in helping bringing Pi Math Contest and this book to life and hope that this book will help many students in their math journeys.

Problems and solution writers:

Adam Tang, Ali Gurel, Andrew Lin, Ata Pir, Brandon Wang, Edwin Xie, Freya Edholm, George Cao, Handong Wang, Hanna Chen, Helen Pang, Isaac Li, Jocelyn Zhu, Jonathan Zhou, Justin Sun, Mason Fang, Matthew Hase-Liu, Mehmet Kaysi, Michael Zhang, Raymond Feng, Richard Spence, Rohan Cherukuri, Shreyas Ramamurthy, Stan Zhang, Stanley Wang, Stephen Xia, Tiger Che, and Victor Hakim.

Giving invaluable feedback:

Ali Ersoz, Freya Edholm, Henry Wang, Justin Stevens, Mehmet Kaysi, and Yalcin Udun.

Editing the book:

Aaron Chen, Ali Gurel, Adam Tang, Aditya Chandrasekhar, Alex Gu, Andrew Chang, Catherine Li, Ethan Lee, George Cao, Henry Wang, Jason Mao, Linus Tang, Olivia Xu, Raina Wu, Rohan Das, Sanya Badhe, Sasidhar Kunapuli, Sejal Rathi, Steven Pan, William Zhao, and Zihongbo Wang.

To The Reader

PiMC individual tests have 25 problems to be solved in 40 minutes. There are four individual tests in this book. Each test starts with an instruction page. Please read the instructions before taking the tests.

The last test is a final round test. It was for invited students who scored high on the first round test. Therefore, the final round problems are overall more difficult than the other tests.

If you want to stimulate an actual testing environment, take the tests in a quite place and time yourself. However, if you cannot solve all the problems within the time limit, you are encouraged to continue working on the remaining problems before seeing their solutions.

After checking your answers, please go through the solutions, especially for the problems that you didn't solve correctly. When you read the solutions, try to understand the motivation behind the steps in the solution, so that you know when to use those ideas in the future.

Enjoy solving problems!

Table of Contents

2019 Fermat	1
Answer Key	7
Solutions	9
2020 Fermat	19
Answer Key	25
Solutions	27
2021 Fermat	37
Answer Key	45
Solutions	47
2019 Fermat Final Round	63
Answer Key	69
Solutions	71

Pi Math Contest VOL 3

2019 Fermat

INSTRUCTIONS

1. This is a twenty-five-question test. Each question has an answer among the numbers 0, 1, 2, ..., 98, 99.

2. SCORING: You will receive 10 points for each correct answer, 1 point for each problem left unanswered, and 0 points for each incorrect answer.

3. No computational aids are permitted other than Ruler and Compass. No calculators are allowed. No problems on the test *require* the use of a calculator.

4. Figures are not necessarily drawn to scale.

5. You will have **40 minutes** to complete the test.

1. What is the value of
$$144 \times \left(\frac{1}{12} + \frac{1}{16}\right)?$$

2. What is the sum of 45% of 20 and 20% of 45?

3. Find the integer closest to 3.08×25.09.

4. Evaluate
$$\sqrt{21 + \sqrt{13 + \sqrt{7 + \sqrt{3 + \sqrt{1}}}}}.$$

5. What is the volume of a cube whose surface area is 54?

6. There are 25 prime numbers less than 100. How many composite numbers are there less than 100?

7. In a classroom, there are 52 students: 29 boys and 23 girls. 42 students wear glasses. What is the fewest number of boys that could be wearing glasses?

8. Alfredo has a right triangle with side lengths 9, 12, and 15. He has another right triangle with side lengths 5, 12, and 13. He glues these two triangles along the edge with length 12 and gets a triangle with lengths 13, 14, and 15. What is the area of this triangle?

9. If n different lines on a plane intersect at 28 different points, what is the smallest possible value of n?

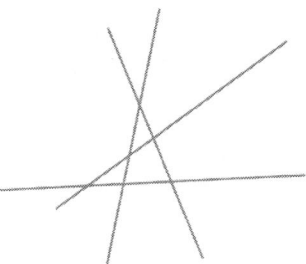

10. What is the remainder when 123456789 is divided by 72?

11. How many positive integers less than 1000 have exactly three positive integer divisors?

12. One day, Al drives from San Francisco to San Diego to have lunch in his favorite restaurant. Unfortunately, it is closed, and he immediately drives back to San Francisco. On the way to San Diego, he drives with an average speed of 72 miles per hour. On the way back, he drives with an average speed of 56 miles per hour. If the trip each way is 504 miles, what is Al's average speed, in miles per hour, for the entire trip?

13. Amanda has 1 quarter, 3 dimes, 5 nickels, and 7 pennies in her pocket. She wants to buy a mango for 77 cents. In how many ways can she pay for the mango using these coins without getting back any change?

14. Two similar triangles have areas 5 and 720. What is the ratio of the perimeter of the larger triangle to the perimeter of the smaller triangle?

15. Bob hires one worker to build four identical houses. To speed up the process, he doubles the number of workers after each house is built. How many weeks will it take to finish building four houses if each worker can build one house in 40 weeks working alone? Assume all workers work at a constant, equal rate.

16. Let $x@y = (x^2 + x) - (y^2 + y) - 1$. For example, $2@1 = 6 - 2 - 1 = 3$. What is
$$(12@11) + (10@9) + \cdots + (2@1)?$$

17. The greatest common factor and the least common multiple of two composite numbers are 11 and 1001, respectively. What is the positive difference between these two composite numbers?

18. In quadrilateral $ABCD$ with different integer side lengths, $AC = 25$, and $\angle ABC = \angle ADC = 90°$. What is the perimeter of $ABCD$?

19. A group of bored children decide to play a game. Each child writes down the number of other children who have the same number of toys as himself or herself. The set of numbers written down is $\{0, 1, 2, 5, 19, 23\}$. Find the smallest possible number of children in the group.

20. From a group of 5 men and 5 women, how many ways are there to choose a committee of 6 people containing strictly more women than men?

21. A cylinder has a radius of 48 and a height of 54. Its volume is half the volume of a hemisphere. What is the radius of the hemisphere?

22. A positive two-digit number N is given. The digits are reversed to form a different two-digit number. If the absolute difference between these two two-digit numbers is less than 40, how many possible values for N are there?

23. What is
$$\lfloor\sqrt{100}\rfloor - \lfloor\sqrt{99}\rfloor + \lfloor\sqrt{98}\rfloor - \lfloor\sqrt{97}\rfloor + \cdots + \lfloor\sqrt{2}\rfloor - \lfloor\sqrt{1}\rfloor?$$

Note: $\lfloor x \rfloor$ denotes the greatest integer less than or equal to x.

24. What are the last two digits of 2^{100}?

25. $\triangle ABC$ is an isosceles triangle with $AB = BC = 1$ and $\angle B = 120°$. Let O be the circumcenter of $\triangle ABC$. Let D be the point on the circumcircle of ABC which is diametrically opposite B. Let E be the intersection point of lines AB and CD, and let F be the intersection point of lines AD and BC. Find the square of the area of $\triangle OEF$.

Test-1 Answer Key

1. 21
2. 18
3. 77
4. 05
5. 27
6. 73
7. 19
8. 84
9. 08
10. 45
11. 11
12. 63
13. 03
14. 12
15. 75
16. 78
17. 66
18. 66
19. 56
20. 55
21. 72
22. 52
23. 05
24. 76
25. 12

Test-1 Solutions

1. What is the value of
$$144 \times \left(\frac{1}{12} + \frac{1}{16}\right)?$$

    Answer (21): Expanding, we get
    $$\frac{144}{12} + \frac{144}{16} = 12 + 9 = 21.$$

2. What is the sum of 45% of 20 and 20% of 45?

    Answer (18): Note that both numbers are same as $\frac{45 \times 20}{100} = 9$. Hence, the answer is $9 + 9 = 18$.

3. Find the integer closest to 3.08×25.09.

    Answer (77): We split each number into its integer part and decimal part before performing the multiplication:
    $$\begin{aligned}(3 + 0.08) \times (25 + 0.09) &= (3 \times 25) + (3 \times 0.09) + (0.08 \times 25) + (0.08 \times 0.09) \\ &= 75 + 0.27 + 2 + 0.0072 \\ &\approx 77.\end{aligned}$$

4. Evaluate
$$\sqrt{21+\sqrt{13+\sqrt{7+\sqrt{3+\sqrt{1}}}}}.$$

Answer (05): We start working our way from the innermost square root:

$$\begin{aligned}
\sqrt{21+\sqrt{13+\sqrt{7+\sqrt{3+\sqrt{1}}}}} &= \sqrt{21+\sqrt{13+\sqrt{7+\sqrt{3+1}}}} \\
&= \sqrt{21+\sqrt{13+\sqrt{7+2}}} \\
&= \sqrt{21+\sqrt{13+3}} \\
&= \sqrt{21+4} \\
&= 05.
\end{aligned}$$

5. What is the volume of a cube whose surface area is 54?

Answer (27): Let a be the side length of the cube. Then its surface area is $6a^2 = 54$. So $a = 3$ and the volume of the cube is $3^3 = 27$.

6. There are 25 prime numbers less than 100. How many composite numbers are there less than 100?

Answer (73): There are 99 positive integers less than 100. Among these, 25 are prime, and one of them (the number 1) is neither prime nor composite. The remaining $99 - 25 - 1 = 73$ are composite numbers.

7. In a classroom, there are 52 students: 29 boys and 23 girls. 42 students wear glasses. What is the fewest number of boys that could be wearing glasses?

Test-1 Solutions   11

Answer (19): The number of boys who wear glasses would be smallest if all the girls wore glasses. If all 23 girls wear glasses, we would still need $42 - 23 = 19$ boys who wear glasses.
Alternative Solution: There are $52 - 42 = 10$ students in class who do not wear glasses. Even if all of them were boys, there would still be at least $29 - 10 = 19$ boys who wear glasses.

8. Alfredo has a right triangle with side lengths 9, 12, and 15. He has another right triangle with side lengths 5, 12, and 13. He glues these two triangles along the edge with length 12 and gets a triangle with lengths 13, 14, and 15. What is the area of this triangle?

   Answer (84): The two right triangles have areas $\dfrac{9 \times 12}{2} = 54$ and $\dfrac{5 \times 12}{2} = 30$. So the combined area is $54 + 30 = 84$. Alternatively, note that the combined area has base 14 and height 12. So its area is $\dfrac{14 \times 12}{2} = 84$. Note that, reversing the steps in this problem, one could also start with the triangle with side lengths 13, 14, 15 and find its area by decomposing it into two right triangles.

9. If n different lines on a plane intersect at 28 different points, what is the smallest possible value of n?

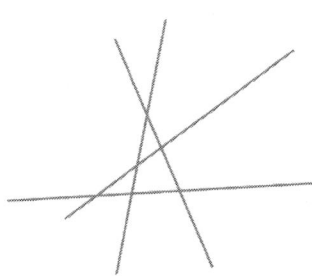

Answer (08): Given n lines, they form the *maximum* number of intersection points when each pair of lines intersects and no three lines intersect at one point. Thus we can count the number of pairs of lines which exist within n lines. This is n choose 2:
$$\binom{n}{2} = \frac{n(n-1)}{2}$$
Solving
$$\frac{n(n-1)}{2} = 28 = \frac{8 \times 7}{2}$$
we find that $n = 08$.

10. What is the remainder when 123456789 is divided by 72?

    Answer (45): Observe that 123456600 is a multiple of 8 and 9, hence a multiple of 72. Subtracting this from the original number, we get 189 which is $2 \times 72 + 45$.

11. How many positive integers less than 1000 have exactly three positive integer divisors?

    Answer (11): To have exactly three positive integer divisors, a number must be of the form p^2 where p is prime. We require that $p^2 < 1000$, so we must have $p < 32$. There are 11 primes less than 32: 2, 3, 5, 7, 11, 13, 17, 19, 23, 29, and 31. Indeed, the valid numbers are
    $$2^2, 3^2, 5^2, 7^2, \ldots, 29^2, 31^2.$$

12. One day, Al drives from San Francisco to San Diego to have lunch in his favorite restaurant. Unfortunately, it is closed, and he immediately drives back to San Francisco. On the way to San Diego, he drives with an average speed of 72 miles per hour. On the way back, he drives with an average speed of 56 miles per hour. If the trip each way is 504 miles, what is Al's average speed, in miles per hour, for the entire trip?

    Answer (63): The round trip takes
    $$\frac{504}{72} + \frac{504}{56} = 7 + 9 = 16 \text{ hours.}$$

He covers a total distance of $504 \times 2 = 1008$ miles. So, his average speed is $\dfrac{1008}{16} = 63$ miles per hour. Note that the average of the numbers 72 and 56 is 64 whereas Al's average speed is less than this. The reason for this is that he is traveling more time with the lesser speed of 56 mph. So his average speed is a little closer to 56 mph than 72 mph.

13. Amanda has 1 quarter, 3 dimes, 5 nickels, and 7 pennies in her pocket. She wants to buy a mango for 77 cents. In how many ways can she pay for the mango using these coins without getting back any change?

    Answer (03): Amanda's coins have a total value of
    $$25 + (3 \times 10) + (5 \times 5) + (7 \times 1) = 87 \text{ cents.}$$
    Thus, we need to find the number of ways for Amanda to keep 10 cents worth of coins. There are 03 ways for Amanda to keep 10 cents: 1 dime, a nickel and 5 pennies, or 2 nickels.

14. Two similar triangles have areas 5 and 720. What is the ratio of the perimeter of the larger triangle to the perimeter of the smaller triangle?

    Answer (12): The ratio of their areas is $720 \div 5 = 12^2$. So, the ratio of the side lengths of the triangles is 12. In particular, each side in the larger triangle is 12 times the corresponding side in the smaller triangle. Hence, the perimeter of the larger triangle is also 12 times the perimeter of the smaller triangle.

15. Bob hires one worker to build four identical houses. To speed up the process, he doubles the number of workers after each house is built. How many weeks will it take to finish building four houses if each worker can build one house in 40 weeks working alone? Assume all workers work at a constant, equal rate.

    Answer (75): The number of workers building first, second, third, and fourth houses will be 1, 2, 4, and 8, respectively. So, successive houses will be built in $\dfrac{40}{1}, \dfrac{40}{2}, \dfrac{40}{4}, \dfrac{40}{8}$ weeks. The answer is
    $$40 + 20 + 10 + 5 = 75.$$

16. Let $x@y = (x^2 + x) - (y^2 + y) - 1$. For example, $2@1 = 6 - 2 - 1 = 3$. What is
$$(12@11) + (10@9) + \cdots + (2@1)?$$

Answer (78): Note that, for $x = y + 1$,
$$x@y = (y+1)^2 + (y+1) - (y^2 + y) - 1 = 2y + 1 = (y+1) + y.$$
So,
$$(12@11) + (10@9) + \cdots + (2@1) = 12 + 11 + 10 + 9 + \cdots + 2 + 1 = \frac{12 \times 13}{2} = 78.$$

17. The greatest common factor and the least common multiple of two composite numbers are 11 and 1001, respectively. What is the positive difference between these two composite numbers?

Answer (66): The prime factorizations of 11 and 1001 are 11^1 and $7^1 \times 11^1 \times 13^1$, respectively.

Letting the two numbers be $m = 7^a 11^b 13^c$ and $n = 7^d 11^e 13^f$ where all exponents are non-negative integers, the given LCM fact tells us that $\max(a,d) = \max(b,e) = \max(c,f) = 1$. The GCD fact tells us that $\min(a,d) = 0$, $\min(b,e) = 1$, and $\min(c,f) = 0$.

Thus, b and e must both be 1, a and d are 0 and 1 (up to ordering), and c and f are 0 and 1 (up to ordering). The two possibilities are that $\{m,n\} = \{77, 143\}$, or $\{11, 1001\}$. However, since m and n are both composite, the latter solution is invalid, so m and n are 77 and 143 (up to order). Their positive difference is $143 - 77 = 66$.

Alternative Solution: Let the numbers be $11 \times a$ and $11 \times b$. The given conditions translate into $GCD(a,b) = 1$ and $LCM(a,b) = 7 \times 13$. Hence, a and b must be 7 and 13. The original numbers are 11×13 and 11×7 and their difference is $11 \times 6 = 66$.

18. In quadrilateral $ABCD$ with different integer side lengths, $AC = 25$, and $\angle ABC = \angle ADC = 90°$. What is the perimeter of $ABCD$?

    Answer (66): Let $AB = a$, $BC = b$, $CD = c$ and $DA = d$. Then by the Pythagorean theorem we have $a^2 + b^2 = c^2 + d^2 = 25^2$. Note that the only positive integer solutions to $x^2 + y^2 = 25^2$ are $(15, 20), (20, 15), (7, 24)$, and $(24, 7)$. Since a, b, c and d are different, we must have $\{a, b, c, d\} = \{15, 20, 7, 24\}$. Hence, the perimeter is $15 + 20 + 7 + 24 = 66$.

19. A group of bored children decide to play a game. Each child writes down the number of other children who have the same number of toys as himself or herself. The set of numbers written down is $\{0, 1, 2, 5, 19, 23\}$. Find the smallest possible number of children in the group.

    Answer (56): If Alice, a child, writes down the number n, then there are exactly $n+1$ children who have the same number of toys as Alice, including herself. Thus, the minimum size of the group is $1 + 2 + 3 + 6 + 20 + 24 = 56$. Note that this is not the only possible group size; for example, if 24 more children are added to the group, each with some number t of toys (where no other child has t toys), then the number 23 will be written an extra 24 times.

20. From a group of 5 men and 5 women, how many ways are there to choose a committee of 6 people containing strictly more women than men?

    Answer (55): There are $\binom{10}{6} = \frac{10!}{4!6!} = 210$ possible committees of size 6, with no restriction. We first count the number of committees with an equal number of men and women. Such a committee has 3 men and 3 women, so the number of such committees equals $\binom{5}{3} \times \binom{5}{3} = 10 \times 10 = 100$.

    Out of the remaining $210 - 100 = 110$ committees containing an unequal number of men and women, exactly half of these committees contains more women than men, by symmetry. The desired answer is $\frac{1}{2} \times 110 = 55$.

    Alternative Solution: The number of women and men in the committee can be $(5,1)$ or $(4,2)$. So, the total number of possibilities is
    $$\binom{5}{5}\binom{5}{1} + \binom{5}{4}\binom{5}{2} = 5 + 5 \cdot 10 = 55.$$

21. A cylinder has a radius of 48 and a height of 54. Its volume is half the volume of a hemisphere. What is the radius of the hemisphere?

   Answer (72): The volume of the cylinder is $\pi \times 48^2 \times 54$. Let r be the radius of the hemisphere. Then the volume of the hemisphere is $\frac{1}{2}\left(\frac{4}{3}\pi r^3\right) = \frac{2}{3}\pi r^3$. The volume of the cylinder is half the volume of the hemisphere, $\frac{1}{3}\pi r^3$. So we must have

$$\frac{1}{3}\pi r^3 = \pi \times 48^2 \times 54$$
$$r^3 = 3 \times 48^2 \times 54$$
$$= 2^9 \times 3^6$$

   So $r = 2^3 \times 3^2 = 72$.

22. A positive two-digit number N is given. The digits are reversed to form a different two-digit number. If the absolute difference between these two two-digit numbers is less than 40, how many possible values for N are there?

   Answer (52): Let $N = 10a + b$ where a and b are digits and let $M = 10b + a$. Note that a and b must be different and non-zero since N and M are different two-digit numbers. The difference $|N - M|$ is $9|a - b|$. For this to be less than 40, we need $|a - b| \leq 4$. If $a < b$, then there are 26 solutions. Four solutions for each of the values $a = 1, 2, 3, 4, 5$, three solutions when $a = 6$, two solutions for $a = 7$, one solution when $a = 8$. By symmetry, we get the same number of solutions when $a > b$. So there are 52 solutions in total.

23. What is
$$\left\lfloor\sqrt{100}\right\rfloor - \left\lfloor\sqrt{99}\right\rfloor + \left\lfloor\sqrt{98}\right\rfloor - \left\lfloor\sqrt{97}\right\rfloor + \cdots + \left\lfloor\sqrt{2}\right\rfloor - \left\lfloor\sqrt{1}\right\rfloor?$$

   Note: $\lfloor x \rfloor$ denotes the greatest integer less than or equal to x.

   Answer (05): Note that, since we are dealing with the greatest integer function, the fractional part of each number can be neglected. Thus, $\lfloor\sqrt{n}\rfloor = \lfloor\sqrt{n-1}\rfloor$ so long as n is not a perfect square. Since k^2 and $(k+1)^2$ have different parities for any integer k, the desired expression simplifies to

$$(10 - 9) + (8 - 7) + (6 - 5) + (4 - 3) + (2 - 1) = 05.$$

24. What are the last two digits of 2^{100}?

   Answer (76): We start with $2^{10} = 1024$ which ends in 24. Squaring both sides we find that 2^{20} ends in 76. Now notice that $76^2 = 5776$ also ends in 76. Hence, all powers of 76 end in 76 as well. In particular $2^{100} = (2^{20})^5$ ends in 76.

25. $\triangle ABC$ is an isosceles triangle with $AB = BC = 1$ and $\angle B = 120°$. Let O be the circumcenter of $\triangle ABC$. Let D be the point on the circumcircle of ABC which is diametrically opposite B. Let E be the intersection point of lines AB and CD, and let F be the intersection point of lines AD and BC. Find the square of the area of $\triangle OEF$.

   Answer (12): We have that DEF is an equilateral triangle with side length $2\sqrt{3}$, and that if T is the intersection of BD and EF, then $DT = 3$ and so $OT = 2$. So, our area is $2\sqrt{3} \times 2 \times \dfrac{1}{2} = 2\sqrt{3}$ and the square of the area is 12.

Pi Math Contest VOL 3

2020 Fermat

INSTRUCTIONS

1. This is a twenty-five-question test. Each question has an answer among the numbers 0, 1, 2, ..., 98, 99.

2. SCORING: You will receive 10 points for each correct answer, 1 point for each problem left unanswered, and 0 points for each incorrect answer.

3. No computational aids are permitted other than Ruler and Compass. No calculators are allowed. No problems on the test *require* the use of a calculator.

4. Figures are not necessarily drawn to scale.

5. You will have **40 minutes** to complete the test.

1. Compute
$$(-3) \times (-2) \times (-1) \times 0 \times 1 \times 2 \times 3.$$

2. Evaluate the following expression:
$$5 \times \left(1 + \frac{3}{1 + \frac{2}{3}}\right).$$

3. Twice a number is equal to 30 more than three-fourths of the original number. What is the number?

4. The product of two integers is 24. What is the largest possible sum of these two integers?

5. The ratio of Mark's age to his father's age is $3:8$. In 12 years, Mark's father will be twice as old as Mark. How many years old is Mark now?

6. A two-digit number is *completely prime* if it is prime, and both of its digits are prime. For example, 37 is completely prime. What is the sum of the smallest and the largest *completely prime* number?

7. Tom eats half of the cookies in a jar. Then, Carol eats half of the remaining cookies. Finally, Alejandro eats half of what was left, leaving only five cookies in the jar. How many cookies were there in the jar at the beginning?

8. Rectangle $ABCD$ has side lengths $AB = 4$ and $BC = 3$. A square $ACKL$ is drawn in the same plane as the rectangle. What is the area of the region outside the rectangle but inside the square?

Test-2
                                                                                                              21

9. Han Solo and Chewbacca have created a scale model of the Millennium Falcon starship. The model has a volume of 6 cubic meters and has a length of 4 meters. If the volume of the actual Millennium Falcon is 2058 cubic meters, what is the length of the actual Millennium Falcon, in meters?

10. A positive integer n less than 100 leaves a remainder of 3 when divided by 4, 2 when divided by 5, and 1 when divided by 6. What is the largest possible value of n?

11. Bart, Lisa, and Maggie share 50 donuts such that:

    - Bart gets more than Lisa and Maggie combined.
    - Lisa gets more than Maggie.

    What is the greatest number of donuts that Maggie could get?

12. Cynthia has a jar containing the same number of pennies, dimes, and quarters. The total value of the coins in the jar is $3.96. How many coins does Cynthia have?

13. The polygon below has eleven sides of length 4 and one side of length 20, and all angles are either 90° or 270°. What is the area of the shaded region?

14. The *Fibonacci sequence* is the sequence $1, 1, 2, 3, 5, 8, 13, \ldots$, where every term after the second is equal to the sum of the two preceding terms. What is the remainder when the 100th term of the Fibonacci sequence is divided by 8?

15. In a school with 100 students, the following table shows the number of students by gender who like the corresponding subject:

	English	Math
Male	42	43
Female	44	45

    How many students like both of the subjects, if each student likes at least one subject?

16. An integer A and prime numbers B and C satisfy the equation
    $$34 \times A + 51 \times B = 6 \times C.$$
    Find $A + B + C$.

17. Coach Comet needs to divide his eight distinguishable reindeer into two teams of four reindeer each. In how many different ways can he do this?

18. Mr. Ruler has a box that measures 3 inches by 4 inches by 12 inches. Loving to measure lengths, Mr. Ruler picks one of the vertices and measures the distances from that vertex to every other vertex of the box. What is the sum of all of the distinct integer lengths (in inches) that he measures?

19. At an office supply store, posters cost $5 each and notebooks cost $4 each. Rahul has $800 to spend on posters and notebooks. How many different combinations of posters and/or notebooks can Rahul buy for exactly $800? (For example, he may buy 200 notebooks, or may buy 20 posters and 175 notebooks)

20. Compute
    $$\left|\lfloor\sqrt[3]{-1}\rfloor\right| + \left|\lfloor\sqrt[3]{-2}\rfloor\right| + \left|\lfloor\sqrt[3]{-3}\rfloor\right| + \ldots + \left|\lfloor\sqrt[3]{-20}\rfloor\right|,$$
    where $\lfloor x \rfloor$ denotes the greatest integer less than or equal to x and $|x|$ denotes the absolute value of x.

21. Rohan has a circular piece of paper. He cuts away an $n°$ sector of the circle and discards it. Then, using the leftover sector of the circle, he tapes the radii together, forming the lateral surface of a cone. If the cone has a height of 4 inches and a radius of 3 inches, what is the remainder when n is divided by 100?

22. Find the integer x that satisfies both of the following equations:
$$x^3 - 29x^2 + 126x - 144 = 0$$
$$2x^3 - 61x^2 + 318x - 144 = 0.$$

23. $ABCDEFGHI$ is a regular nonagon. How many trapezoids are there such that all four vertices of the trapezoid are vertices of $ABCDEFGHI$? One example is $ABCI$.

24. What is the remainder when 18^{17} is divided by 100?

25. Equilateral triangle ABC has side length 6. Let D be the point on segment $\overline{BC}$ such that $BD = 4$. The circle passing through points A, B, and C intersects line AD at A and at another point E. The length of DE can be expressed in simplest radical form as $\dfrac{a\sqrt{b}}{c}$, where a, b, and c are positive integers. What is $a + b + c$?

Test-2 Answer Key

1. 0
2. 14
3. 24
4. 25
5. 18
6. 96
7. 40
8. 19
9. 28
10. 67
11. 11
12. 33
13. 72
14. 3
15. 74
16. 19
17. 35
18. 37
19. 41
20. 51
21. 44
22. 24
23. 54
24. 68
25. 18

Test-2 Solutions

1. Compute
$$(-3) \times (-2) \times (-1) \times 0 \times 1 \times 2 \times 3.$$

   Answer (0): Since one of the factors is 0, the whole product is $\boxed{0}$.

2. Evaluate the following expression:
$$5 \times \left(1 + \frac{3}{1 + \frac{2}{3}}\right).$$

   Answer (14): $5 \times \left(1 + \frac{3}{1+\frac{2}{3}}\right) = 5 \times \left(1 + \frac{3}{5/3}\right) = 5 \times \left(1 + \frac{9}{5}\right) = 5 \times \frac{14}{5} = 14.$

3. Twice a number is equal to 30 more than three-fourths of the original number. What is the number?

   Answer (24): Let x be the value of this number. The question statement tells us $2x = 30 + \frac{3}{4}x$. Solving, we have $\frac{5}{4}x = 30$, so our number $x = 24$.

4. The product of two integers is 24. What is the largest possible sum of these two integers?

   Answer (25): To make the sum positive, we let the two integers be positive. Then the possibilities for the sum are $1+24, 2+12, 3+8, 4+6$ or $25, 14, 11,$ and 10. The largest of these is 25.

Alternatively, note that the sum of two numbers with a fixed product increases as the numbers get further away from each other. Hence, the sum would be largest when the numbers are 1 and 24.

5. The ratio of Mark's age to his father's age is 3 : 8. In 12 years, Mark's father will be twice as old as Mark. How many years old is Mark now?

   Answer (18): Let Mark's and his father's ages be $3x$ and $8x$, respectively. In 12 years, Mark will be $3x+12$ and his father will be $8x+12$. Thus, we have $8x+12 = 2(3x+12)$. Solving this, we get $x = 6$. Mark's current age is therefore $3x = 18$.

6. A two-digit number is *completely prime* if it is prime, and both of its digits are prime. For example, 37 is completely prime. What is the sum of the smallest and the largest *completely prime* number?

   Answer (96): Since 2, 3, 5, and 7 are the only prime digits, a *completely prime* number must consist of only these digits. 22 is not prime, but 23 is prime, so it is the smallest such number. The largest completely prime number is 73 (77 and 75 are not prime). Their sum is $23 + 73 = 96$.

7. Tom eats half of the cookies in a jar. Then, Carol eats half of the remaining cookies. Finally, Alejandro eats half of what was left, leaving only five cookies in the jar. How many cookies were there in the jar at the beginning?

   Answer (40): Working backwards, note that each person eats the same number of cookies as they leave in the jar. Hence, the number of cookies before each person visits is double the number of cookies after their visit. Therefore, at the beginning there were $5 \times 2^3 = 40$ cookies in the jar.

8. Rectangle $ABCD$ has side lengths $AB = 4$ and $BC = 3$. A square $ACKL$ is drawn in the same plane as the rectangle. What is the area of the region outside the rectangle but inside the square?

   Answer (19): Note that $ACKL$ is a 5 by 5 square and half of the rectangle $ABCD$

is enclosed entirely within the square $ACKL$. Thus, the area outside the rectangle but inside the squares is simply the area of the square minus half the area of the rectangle. So, the answer is $5 \times 5 - \dfrac{3 \times 4}{2} = 25 - 6 = 19$.

9. Han Solo and Chewbacca have created a scale model of the Millennium Falcon starship. The model has a volume of 6 cubic meters and has a length of 4 meters. If the volume of the actual Millennium Falcon is 2058 cubic meters, what is the length of the actual Millennium Falcon, in meters?

    Answer (28): The volume of the actual Millennium Falcon is $\dfrac{2058}{6} = 343$ times the volume of the model, which is equal to $7 \times 7 \times 7$. So the ratio of the length of the actual Falcon to the model Falcon is 7. Hence, the length of the actual Falcon is $4 \times 7 = 28$ meters.

10. A positive integer n less than 100 leaves a remainder of 3 when divided by 4, 2 when divided by 5, and 1 when divided by 6. What is the largest possible value of n?

    Answer (67): Observe that $n = 7$ satisfies the given conditions. Then $n - 7$ must have remainder 0 when divided by 4, 5, and 6. Hence, $n - 7$ must be a multiple of $lcm(4, 5, 6) = 60$. Since n is less than 100, the largest value it can take is $7 + 60 = 67$.

11. Bart, Lisa, and Maggie share 50 donuts such that:
    - Bart gets more than Lisa and Maggie combined.
    - Lisa gets more than Maggie.

    What is the greatest number of donuts that Maggie could get?

    Answer (11): Since Bart got more than the rest combined, he got more than half, or at least 26 donuts. That means Lisa and Maggie shared at most 24 donuts. Since Maggie got less than Lisa, she got less than half of these donuts, or at most $\boxed{11}$ donuts. Note that Maggie could indeed get 11 donuts if Lisa got 13 and Bart got 26 donuts.

12. Cynthia has a jar containing the same number of pennies, dimes, and quarters. The total value of the coins in the jar is $3.96. How many coins does Cynthia have?

Answer (33): Let the number of each type of coins be n. Then we have

$$n + 10n + 25n = 36n = 396,$$

so $n = 11$. Therefore, Cynthia has $3n = 33$ coins.

Alternatively, since we have the same number of each type, we can group the coins where each group contains a penny, a dime, and a quarter. Each group is worth 36 cents and the jar has coins worth $396 = 36 \times 11$ cents, so we must have 11 groups, and 33 coins.

13. The polygon below has eleven sides of length 4 and one side of length 20, and all angles are either 90° or 270°. What is the area of the shaded region?

Answer (72): Split the polygon in half along the vertical line of symmetry. Then we can directly compute the areas of each of the three triangles in each half to get

$$2\left(\frac{1}{2} \cdot 4 \cdot 2 + \frac{1}{2} \cdot 4 \cdot 6 + \frac{1}{2} \cdot 4 \cdot 10\right) = 72.$$

Alternatively, note that the shaded region has half the area of the polygon, whose area can be decomposed into nine 4×4 squares. Hence, the answer is $\dfrac{9 \times 4 \times 4}{2} = 72$.

14. The *Fibonacci sequence* is the sequence $1, 1, 2, 3, 5, 8, 13, \ldots$, where every term after the second is equal to the sum of the two preceding terms. What is the remainder when the 100th term of the Fibonacci sequence is divided by 8?

Answer (3): The remainders when the terms are divided by 8 are

$$1, 1, 2, 3, 5, 0, 5, 5, 2, 7, 1, 0, 1, 1, 2, 3, 4 \ldots$$

After 12 terms, the remainders repeat themselves. Since 100 is 4 more than a multiple of 12, the desired remainder is the same as the 4th remainder on the list above, which is $\boxed{3}$.

15. In a school with 100 students, the following table shows the number of students by gender who like the corresponding subject:

	English	Math
Male	42	43
Female	44	45

How many students like both of the subjects, if each student likes at least one subject?

Answer (74): Suppose that there are M males and F females. Then $M + F = 100$. Also, we have

$$M = 42 + 43 - (\# \text{ males that like both})$$
$$F = 44 + 45 - (\# \text{ females that like both}).$$

Adding the two equations, we get

$$100 = 174 - (\# \text{ students that like both}),$$

so our answer is 74.

Alternatively, note that 86 students like English, whereas 88 students like Math. This gives $86 + 88 = 174$ students liking at least one subject. The actual number of students (all of whom like at least one subject) is 100. Thus the extra 74 is due to the students who like both subjects.

16. An integer A and prime numbers B and C satisfy the equation

$$34 \times A + 51 \times B = 6 \times C.$$

Find $A + B + C$.

Answer (19): Note that the left hand side is a multiple of 17. Therefore, $6 \times C$ is a multiple of 17. We conclude that C is a multiple of 17 as well. But C is prime so it must be 17. Similarly, note that $34 \times A$ and $6 \times C$ are both even numbers. Hence $51 \times B$ must be even, which implies that B is even as well. Since B is prime, it must be 2. Substituting $B = 2$ and $C = 17$ in the equation, we find that $A = 0$ and $A + B + C = 0 + 2 + 17 = 19$.

17. Coach Comet needs to divide his eight distinguishable reindeer into two teams of four reindeer each. In how many different ways can he do this?

    Answer (35): Choosing any set of 4 reindeer to make one team automatically forces the remaining 4 reindeer to comprise the second team. There are $\binom{8}{4} = 70$ ways to choose the first 4 reindeer. However, each grouping has been counted twice; not choosing any of a group of four reindeer leads to the same division as choosing all of them. Thus, there are actually $70 \div 2 = 35$ ways Coach Comet can split the reindeer.

18. Mr. Ruler has a box that measures 3 inches by 4 inches by 12 inches. Loving to measure lengths, Mr. Ruler picks one of the vertices and measures the distances from that vertex to every other vertex of the box. What is the sum of all of the distinct integer lengths (in inches) that he measures?

    Answer (37): Select a vertex. The edges coming from the vertex have lengths of 3, 4, and 12. The diagonals along each face with the vertex as an endpoint have lengths of $\sqrt{3^2 + 4^2} = 5$, $\sqrt{3^2 + 12^2} = 3\sqrt{17}$, and $\sqrt{4^2 + 12^2} = 4\sqrt{10}$. Finally, the space diagonal with the vertex as as an endpoint has length of $\sqrt{3^2 + 4^2 + 12^2} = 13$. The sum of the integer lengths is hence $3 + 4 + 5 + 12 + 13 = 37$.

19. At an office supply store, posters cost $5 each and notebooks cost $4 each. Rahul has $800 to spend on posters and notebooks. How many different combinations of posters and/or notebooks can Rahul buy for exactly $800? (For example, he may buy 200 notebooks, or may buy 20 posters and 175 notebooks)

    Answer (41): Let p be the number of posters and n the number of notebooks that Rahul buys. We want to find the number of non-negative integer solutions (p, n) to the equation $5p + 4n = 800$. We observe that n must be divisible by 5, by taking the equation modulo 5. Similarly, we also observe that p must be divisible by 4.

    Let $p = 4x$ and $n = 5y$ for non-negative integers x and y. Then we have $5(4x) + 4(5y) = 800 \iff 20x + 20y = 800 \iff x + y = 40$. The number of non-negative integer solutions to $x + y = 40$ is 41.

20. Compute
$$\left|\lfloor\sqrt[3]{-1}\rfloor\right| + \left|\lfloor\sqrt[3]{-2}\rfloor\right| + \left|\lfloor\sqrt[3]{-3}\rfloor\right| + \ldots + \left|\lfloor\sqrt[3]{-20}\rfloor\right|,$$
where $\lfloor x \rfloor$ denotes the greatest integer less than or equal to x and $|x|$ denotes the absolute value of x.

Answer (51): Note that the floor of $\sqrt[3]{-1}$ is -1, the floor of $\sqrt[3]{-2}$ to $\sqrt[3]{-8}$ are all -2, and the floor of $\sqrt[3]{-9}$ to $\sqrt[3]{-20}$ are all -3. Thus, the expression becomes
$$1 + 7 \times 2 + 12 \times 3 = 51.$$

21. Rohan has a circular piece of paper. He cuts away an $n°$ sector of the circle and discards it. Then, using the leftover sector of the circle, he tapes the radii together, forming the lateral surface of a cone. If the cone has a height of 4 inches and a radius of 3 inches, what is the remainder when n is divided by 100?

Answer (44): Since the cone has a height of 4 and radius of 3, the slant height is $\sqrt{3^2 + 4^2} = 5$. The radius of the sector equals the slant height of the cone, so the radius of the paper is 5. We also know that the arc length of the sector is equal to the circumference of the base of the cone. Since n is the degree measure of the paper that was cut away, the degree measure of the sector is $360 - n$. Thus, we can set up the equation $\frac{360-n}{360} \times 2\pi \times 5 = 2\pi \times 3$. Solving, $n = 144$, and the answer is 44.

22. Find the integer x that satisfies both of the following equations:
$$x^3 - 29x^2 + 126x - 144 = 0$$
$$2x^3 - 61x^2 + 318x - 144 = 0.$$

Answer (24): We are given that there is one integer x which satisfies both of the cubic equations. If we multiply the first cubic equation by 2, then subtract the second equation, we obtain:
$$2(x^3 - 29x^2 + 126x - 144) - (2x^3 - 61x^2 + 318x - 144) = 3x^2 - 66x - 144 = 0$$
$$\Rightarrow x^2 - 22x - 48 = 0$$

Note that a solution x to the above quadratic does not imply that x is a solution to both cubics; however the converse is true (namely, if x is a solution to both cubics, then x is a solution to the quadratic $x^2 - 22x - 48 = 0$).

The quadratic factors to $(x-24)(x+2) = 0$, so $x = 24$ or $x = -2$. Checking, we see that $x = -2$ does not satisfy the first cubic, but $x = 24$ satisfies both equations, so $x = 24$.

23. $ABCDEFGHI$ is a regular nonagon. How many trapezoids are there such that all four vertices of the trapezoid are vertices of $ABCDEFGHI$? One example is $ABCI$.

    Answer (54): Draw all diagonals of the polygon. There are 9 sets of 4 parallel segments: for each edge, there are 3 diagonals parallel to it. For each set of 4 parallel segments, choosing two of them defines a unique trapezoid; as none of them are rectangles, no double-counting happens. Therefore, the total number of trapezoids is $9 \times \binom{4}{2} = 54$.

24. What is the remainder when 18^{17} is divided by 100?

    Answer (68): We will use Chinese Remainder Theorem: First find the remainders of 18^{17} when divided by 4 and 25, respectively and then combine these to find its remainder when divided by 100. First, note that since 18 is even, 18^{17} is a multiple of 4. Next, observe that $18^2 = 324 \equiv -1 \pmod{25}$. Hence, $18^{16} \equiv (-1)^8 \equiv 1 \pmod{25}$ and $18^{17} \equiv 18 \pmod{25}$. Since 18^{17} has remainder 18 when divided by 25, it must have one of the following remainders when divided by 100:

    $$18,\ 18+25,\ 18+50,\ 18+75.$$

    Among these, only $18 + 50 = 68$ is a multiple of 4.

25. Equilateral triangle ABC has side length 6. Let D be the point on segment $\overline{BC}$ such that $BD = 4$. The circle passing through points A, B, and C intersects line AD at A and at another point E. The length of DE can be expressed in simplest radical form as $\dfrac{a\sqrt{b}}{c}$, where a, b, and c are positive integers. What is $a + b + c$?

    Answer (18): We want to use Power of a Point, so we should find the length of AD. Let M be the foot of the altitude from A to BC. Then AMB is a $30-60-90$

triangle, so $AM = 3\sqrt{3}$, and $BM = 3$, so $MD = 4 - 3 = 1$. Therefore, by the Pythagorean Theorem, $AD = \sqrt{(3\sqrt{3})^2 + 1^2} = \sqrt{28}$. Now, by Power of a Point, $AD \cdot DE = BD \cdot DC$, so $DE = \frac{BD \cdot DC}{AD} = \frac{4 \cdot 2}{\sqrt{28}} = \frac{4\sqrt{7}}{7}$ for an answer of $4 + 7 + 7 = 18$.

Pi Math Contest VOL 3

2021 Fermat

INSTRUCTIONS

1. This is a twenty-five-question test. Each question has an answer among the numbers 0, 1, 2, ..., 98, 99.

2. SCORING: You will receive 10 points for each correct answer, 1 point for each problem left unanswered, and 0 points for each incorrect answer.

3. No computational aids are permitted other than Ruler and Compass. No calculators are allowed. No problems on the test *require* the use of a calculator.

4. Figures are not necessarily drawn to scale.

5. You will have **40 minutes** to complete the test.

1. Simplify $\dfrac{20^{21}}{20^{20}}$.

2. What is
$$\dfrac{\left(\frac{7}{3}+\frac{5}{6}\right)}{\left(\frac{1}{8}+\frac{2}{3}\right)}?$$

3. Charlie took a test with two parts; Reading with 60 questions and Math with 40 questions. He scored 55% on the Reading part and 90% on the Math part. What is his overall percentage score, assuming each of the 100 questions have equal weight?

4. Raymond has squares with side length 2 inches, while Shreyas has squares with side length 1 foot. What is the least number of squares Raymond needs to completely cover one of Shreyas's squares?

5. If Alice takes 8 minutes to complete a math test and it takes Hanna 12 minutes to complete the same math test, how long, in minutes, will it take them to finish 5 tests while working together? Assume all tests have the same length.

6. A two-digit number is added to the number formed by reversing its digits. There is a unique prime p that divides all such sums. What is the remainder when p^4 is divided by 100?

7. Steve is standing right next to a flagpole in the afternoon. After careful measurements, Steve realizes that the flagpole is 8 yards tall. If the shadow of the flagpole is 12 feet long and Steve is 5 feet and 6 inches tall, how long is Steve's shadow, in inches?

8. Michelle flips a fair coin 5 times. Let $\dfrac{m}{n}$ be the probability that she gets more heads than tails, where m and n are relatively prime positive integers. Find $m+n$.

9. Let x and y be real numbers that satisfy
$$x^2 - y^2 = 100,$$
$$x + y = 50.$$

   What is $x + 2y$?

10. A 5-digit number is called *halloweenish* if it has exactly three consecutive 6's. For example, 66636 and 16667 are *halloweenish* numbers but 66664 and 66366 are not. What is the remainder when the total number of *halloweenish* numbers is divided by 66?

11. Let
$$N = \sqrt{2021\sqrt{2021\sqrt{2021\sqrt{\cdots}}}}$$

   What are the last two-digits of N?

12. Justin randomly selects two different integers from the set $\{1, 2, 3, \ldots, 9, 10\}$. Let $\frac{m}{n}$ be the probability that the product is divisible by 10, where m and n are relatively prime positive integers. What is $m + n$?

13. For how many integers n between 1 and 100, inclusive, is $n^{n/2}$ an integer?

14. Let a and b be real numbers that satisfy
$$a^2 + b^2 = 49 + 2ab = 121 - 2ab.$$

   What is $|a^2 - b^2|$?

15. Let ω be a circle with radius 4. Two points, A and B, are chosen uniformly at random on the circumference of ω. The probability that $AB \leq 4\sqrt{3}$ can be expressed in the form $\frac{m}{n}$, where m and n are relatively prime positive integers. What is $m + n$?

16. How many of the first 2021 positive integers have exactly 9 positive factors?

17. A Clash Royale player has an unlimited supply of zaps, logs, and giant snowballs. Zaps do 7 damage, logs do 8 damage, and snowballs do 5 damage to towers. In a special game mode, the only way to take a tower is to deal damage to the tower using the available spells to make its health exactly 0. What is the largest integer amount of health a tower can have that cannot be taken in this game mode?

18. A circle O has radius 8. Another circle P intersects O at A and B. If the arc AB measures 60 degrees with respect to O and 90 degrees with respect to P, then what is the square of the radius of P?

19. Let a and b be distinct real numbers that satisfy
$$(5+a-b)^2 - (5-a+b)^2 = (4+a+b)^2 - (4-a-b)^2.$$
What is $\left(\frac{a}{b}\right)^2$?

20. In chess, a bishop can attack a piece that is on the same diagonal as itself. A king can attack any piece that is in any one of the 8 adjacent spots as itself. If m is the maximum number of kings you can place on an 8×8 chessboard such that no king can attack each other, and n is the maximum number of bishops you can place on a different 8×8 chessboard such that no bishop can attack each other, what is $m + n$? The diagram below shows how the bishop and king attack on the chessboard, with B denoting the bishop and K denoting the king.

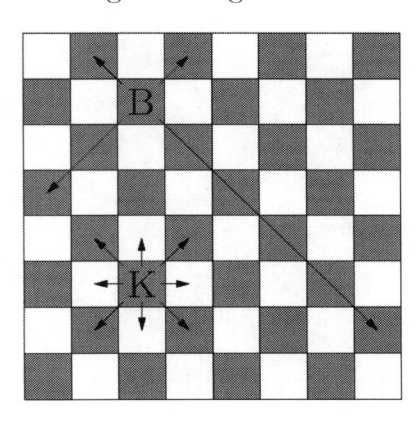

21. Let p, q, and r be primes satisfying
$$3p + q = r^2 - 30.$$
What is the sum of all possible values of $p + q + r$?

22. In $\triangle ABC$, $AB = 8$ and $AC = 12$. If M is the midpoint of segment $\overline{AC}$ and $BM = 6$, then BC can be written in the form $m\sqrt{n}$, where n is not divisible by the square of any prime. What is the value of mn?

23. Let r, s, and t be the solutions of the equation
$$x^3 - 3x^2 - 6x + 2 = 0.$$
What is $r^3 + s^3 + t^3$?

24. A semicircle ω with center O has diameter $AB = 2$. A smaller semicircle ω_1 with center O_1 and passing through O is inscribed in ω. Another semicircle ω_2 whose center O_2 lies on $\overline{AB}$ is drawn such that it passes through A and it is externally tangent to ω_1. If the radius of ω_2 is $\frac{a-\sqrt{b}}{c}$, such that a, b, c are positive integers and b is not divisible by the square of any prime, what is $a + b + c$?

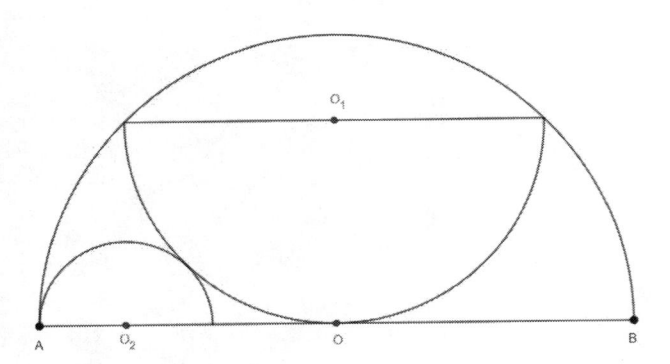

25. Two distinct numbers a and b are selected from $\{1, 2, 3, ..., 9\}$. What is the number of possible distinct values of $\text{lcm}(a, b)$?

Test-3 Answer Key

1. 20
2. 4
3. 69
4. 36
5. 24
6. 41
7. 33
8. 3
9. 74
10. 45
11. 21
12. 58
13. 55
14. 77
15. 5
16. 13
17. 11
18. 32
19. 81
20. 30
21. 22
22. 20
23. 75
24. 6
25. 26

Test-3 Solutions

1. Simplify $\dfrac{20^{21}}{20^{20}}$.

   Answer (20): We can cancel out 20^{20} from the numerator and denominator to get 20 in the end.

2. What is
$$\frac{\left(\frac{7}{3} + \frac{5}{6}\right)}{\left(\frac{1}{8} + \frac{2}{3}\right)}?$$

   Answer (4): Combining the fractions in the numerator and denominator by taking a common denominator, we can simplify this to
$$\frac{\left(\frac{7}{3} + \frac{5}{6}\right)}{\left(\frac{1}{8} + \frac{2}{3}\right)} = \frac{\left(\frac{14+5}{6}\right)}{\left(\frac{3+16}{24}\right)} = \frac{\frac{19}{6}}{\frac{19}{24}}$$
$$= \frac{19}{6} \cdot \frac{24}{19} = \frac{24}{6} = 4.$$

3. Charlie took a test with two parts; Reading with 60 questions and Math with 40 questions. He scored 55% on the Reading part and 90% on the Math part. What is his overall percentage score, assuming each of the 100 questions have equal weight?

   Answer (69): Since Charlie answered $0.55 \cdot 60 = 33$ of the Reading questions and $0.90 \cdot 40 = 36$ of Math questions correctly, his total score is $33 + 36 = 69$ out of 100, so his percentage is 69.

4. Raymond has squares with side length 2 inches, while Shreyas has squares with side length 1 foot. What is the least number of squares Raymond needs to completely cover one of Shreyas's squares?

Answer (36):

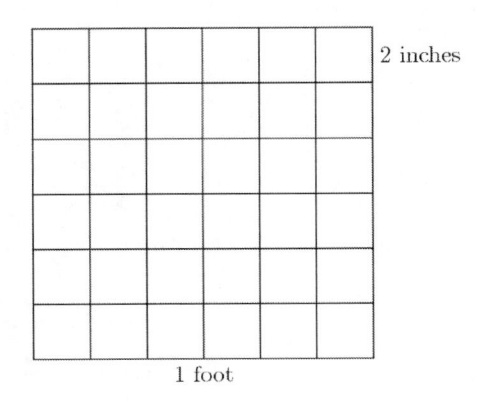

[A 6×6 grid is shown, labeled "2 inches" on the side and "1 foot" at the bottom.]

The area of one of Raymond's squares is $2^2 = 4$ square inches, and the area of one of Shreyas's squares is $12^2 = 144$ square inches, so the number of squares needed is $\frac{144}{4} = 36$.

5. If Alice takes 8 minutes to complete a math test and it takes Hanna 12 minutes to complete the same math test, how long, in minutes, will it take them to finish 5 tests while working together? Assume all tests have the same length.

Answer (24): After x minutes, Alice will have completed $\frac{x}{8}$ of the test while Hanna will have completed $\frac{x}{12}$ of the test. In total, they will have completed

$$\frac{x}{8} + \frac{x}{12} = \frac{5x}{24}$$

of the test. Thus, if they finish 5 tests together in x minutes, we must have

$$\frac{5x}{24} = 5 \implies x = 24.$$

Alternate Solution: In 24 minutes (convenient number to start with since it is a multiple of both 8 and 12), Alice can finish $\frac{24}{8} = 3$ tests while Hanna can finish $\frac{24}{12} = 2$ tests. Hence, they can finish 5 tests together in 24 minutes.

Test-3 Solutions

6. A two-digit number is added to the number formed by reversing its digits. There is a unique prime p that divides all such sums. What is the remainder when p^4 is divided by 100?

   Answer (41): Note that the sum can be written as
   $$(10a + b) + (10b + a) = 11a + 11b = 11(a+b)$$
   which is divisible by 11. Since $11^4 = 14641$, the answer is 41.

   Alternate Solution: We find the sums for two different examples and look for a common prime factor of the sums: For example, starting with the two digit number 12, we get $12 + 21 = 33$. Starting with 13, we get $13 + 31 = 44$. The only common prime factor of 33 and 44 is 11. Hence, $p = 11$. Then $p^4 = 121^2$ has the same remainder as $21^2 = 441$ when divided by 100, so the answer is 41.

7. Steve is standing right next to a flagpole in the afternoon. After careful measurements, Steve realizes that the flagpole is 8 yards tall. If the shadow of the flagpole is 12 feet long and Steve is 5 feet and 6 inches tall, how long is Steve's shadow, in inches?

   Answer (33):

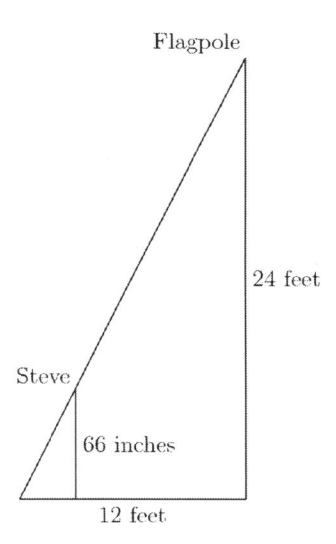

   Using similar triangles, the ratio of the height of an object to the object's shadow length is constant at the same time of day. So, we have
   $$\frac{\text{shadow length of flagpole}}{\text{height of flagpole}} = \frac{\text{shadow length of Steve}}{\text{height of Steve}}.$$

Now we perform unit conversions. Recall that 1 yard is 3 feet, so the flagpole is 24 feet tall, yet its shadow is only 12 feet long, which is half its height. Additionally, since 1 foot is 12 inches, Steve is 66 inches tall. So, his shadow must be half this size, which is 33 inches.

8. Michelle flips a fair coin 5 times. Let $\frac{m}{n}$ be the probability that she gets more heads than tails, where m and n are relatively prime positive integers. Find $m + n$.

   Answer (3): The total number of ways to flip 5 coins is $2^5 = 32$, since any flip has two choices: either heads or tails. We proceed with casework on the number of heads. Note that H stands for heads and T for tails.

   Case 1. She flips 5 heads and 0 tails. There is only 1 way to do this since they are all heads.

   Case 2. She flips 4 heads and 1 tail. There are 5 ways to do this, depending on where the tail is:

   $$\text{THHHH, HTHHH, HHTHH, HHHTH, HHHHT.}$$

   Case 3. She flips 3 heads and 2 tails. There are $\binom{5}{2} = 10$ ways to do this:

   $$\begin{array}{ccccc} \text{TTHHH} & \text{THTHH} & \text{THHTH} & \text{THHHT} & \text{HTTHH} \\ \text{HTHTH} & \text{HTHHT} & \text{HHTTH} & \text{HHTHT} & \text{HHHTT} \end{array}$$

   All other cases have more tails than heads. Therefore, there are $1 + 5 + 10 = 16$ ways that she flips more heads than tails, giving a probability of $\frac{16}{32} = \frac{1}{2}$, and an answer of $1 + 2 = 3$.

   Alternate Solution: By Symmetry, the probability of flipping more heads than tails is equal to the probability of flipping more tails than heads. Since the number of heads and tails can never be equal in 5 flips, the probability is simply $\frac{1}{2}$, so the answer is 3.

9. Let x and y be real numbers that satisfy

   $$x^2 - y^2 = 100,$$
   $$x + y = 50.$$

What is $x + 2y$?

Answer (74): Using difference of squares, we have

$$\begin{aligned} (x+y)(x-y) &= x^2 - y^2 \\ 50(x-y) &= 100 \\ x - y &= 2. \end{aligned}$$

Thus, $x + y = 50$ and $x - y = 2$. Adding the two equations yields $2x = 52$, so $x = 26$. Then $x + y = 50$ gives us $y = 24$. Finally,

$$x + 2y = 26 + 2 \cdot 24 = 74.$$

10. A 5-digit number is called *halloweenish* if it has exactly three consecutive 6's. For example, 66636 and 16667 are *halloweenish* numbers but 66664 and 66366 are not. What is the remainder when the total number of *halloweenish* numbers is divided by 66?

    Answer (45): If the three 6's are the first 3 digits, then there are 9 choices for the 4th digit (it can't be a 6) and 10 choices for the last digit.

    If the three 6's are the middle 3 digits, then there are 8 choices for the first digit (it can't be 0 or 6) and 9 choices for the last digit.

    Finally, if the three 6's are the last 3 digits then there are 9 choices for the first digit and 9 choices for the second digit.

    Hence, the total number of *halloweenish* numbers is

    $$9 \cdot 10 + 9 \cdot 8 + 9 \cdot 9 = 243.$$

    This is $3 \cdot 66 + 45$, so the answer is 45.

11. Let

$$N = \sqrt{2021\sqrt{2021\sqrt{2021\sqrt{\cdots}}}}$$

What are the last two-digits of N?

Answer (21): Notice that
$$N = 2021^{\frac{1}{2}} \cdot 2021^{\frac{1}{4}} \cdot 2021^{\frac{1}{8}} \cdot \ldots = 2021^{\frac{1}{2}+\frac{1}{4}+\frac{1}{8}+\cdots} = 2021^1 = 2021.$$

The last two digits are 21.

Alternate Solution: Using the repeating pattern of N, notice that
$$N^2 = 2021\sqrt{2021\sqrt{2021\sqrt{\ldots}}} = 2021N.$$

Since $N^2 = 2021N$, we must have either $N = 0$ or $N = 2021$. Since N is positive, we conclude that it is 2021.

12. Justin randomly selects two different integers from the set $\{1, 2, 3, \ldots, 9, 10\}$. Let $\frac{m}{n}$ be the probability that the product is divisible by 10, where m and n are relatively prime positive integers. What is $m + n$?

Answer (58): The total number of pairs is
$$\binom{10}{2} = \frac{10 \cdot 9}{2} = 45.$$

Let's find out how many of these pairs give a product that is a multiple of 10:

Any number paired with 10 gives a product divisible by 10. This gives 9 pairs. Furthermore, an even number paired with 5 will also yield a product that is a multiple of 10. Because there are 4 even numbers less than 10 (we do not count 10 because it was already counted in the first case), this gives 4 additional cases. Thus, there are $9 + 4 = 13$ desired pairs. The probability is $\frac{13}{45}$ and the answer is $13 + 45 = 58$.

13. For how many integers n between 1 and 100, inclusive, is $n^{n/2}$ an integer?

Answer (55): All even numbers n work, as then the exponent, $n/2$, is a positive integer. There are 50 of these. If n is odd, then n must be a square in order for $n^{n/2} = (\sqrt{n})^n$ to be an integer. There are 5 odd squares less than or equal to 100. The number of desired n is thus $50 + 5 = 55$.

14. Let a and b be real numbers that satisfy
$$a^2 + b^2 = 49 + 2ab = 121 - 2ab.$$
What is $|a^2 - b^2|$?

Answer (77): The first equation yields
$$a^2 - 2ab + b^2 = 49 \implies (a-b)^2 = 49 \implies |a-b| = 7.$$

Similarly, the second equation yields
$$a^2 + 2ab + b^2 = 121 \implies (a+b) = 11^2 \implies |a+b| = 11.$$

Finally, we have
$$|a^2 - b^2| = |a-b| \cdot |a+b| = 7 \cdot 11 = 77.$$

15. Let ω be a circle with radius 4. Two points, A and B, are chosen uniformly at random on the circumference of ω. The probability that $AB \leq 4\sqrt{3}$ can be expressed in the form $\frac{m}{n}$, where m and n are relatively prime positive integers. What is $m + n$?

Answer (5):

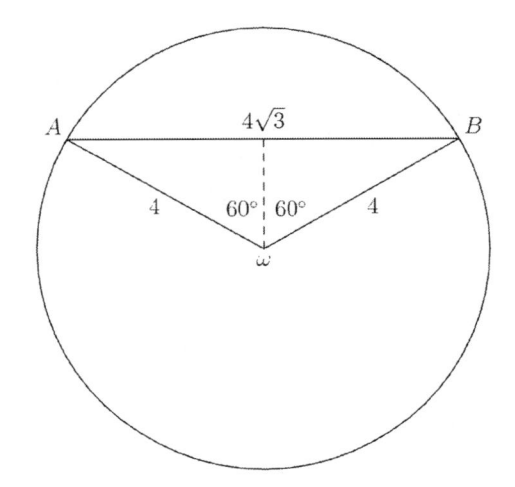

If $AB = 4\sqrt{3}$, then the angle of the minor arc $\stackrel{\frown}{AB}$ is $120°$ since we can form two 30-60-90 triangles by dropping an altitude, as shown in the diagram. Pick any point A on the circle. Then, for $\stackrel{\frown}{AB} \leq 120°$, B must either be within 120 degrees to the left of A or the right of A. This spans a total of 240 degree part of the circumference, so the probability is $\frac{240}{360} = \frac{2}{3}$, and the answer is $2 + 3 = 5$.

16. How many of the first 2021 positive integers have exactly 9 positive factors?

    Answer (13): Recall that if $n = p_1^{\alpha_1} \ldots p_k^{\alpha_k}$ is the prime factorization of a number n, then the number of positive factors of n is $(p_1 + 1) \cdots (p_k + 1)$.

    Hence, if the number of positive factors is 9, then the prime factorization must be in the form of either p^8 or $p^2 q^2$.

    Case 1: $n = p^2 q^2$. Note that since $n \leq 2021 < 45^2$, we have $pq = \sqrt{n} < 45$. So, we just need to count the number of unordered pairs of distinct primes p, q such that $pq < 45$. The possibilities are:

    $$(2,3), (2,5), (2,7), \ldots, (2,19); \ (3,5), (3,7), \ldots, (3,13); \ (5,7).$$

    There are 12 numbers in this case.

    Case 2: $n = p^8$. The only possible p in this case is 2.

    Therefore, the answer is $12 + 1 = 13$.

17. A Clash Royale player has an unlimited supply of zaps, logs, and giant snowballs. Zaps do 7 damage, logs do 8 damage, and snowballs do 5 damage to towers. In a special game mode, the only way to take a tower is to deal damage to the tower using the available spells to make its health exactly 0. What is the largest integer amount of health a tower can have that cannot be taken in this game mode?

    Answer (11): We want to find the largest integer that cannot be written as a sum of 5's, 7's, and 8's.

    Note that 11 cannot be obtained this way. On the other hand, the numbers

    $$12 = 5 + 7, \ 13 = 5 + 8, \ 14 = 7 + 7, \ 15 = 7 + 8, \text{ and } 16 = 8 + 8$$

    can all be written using 5's, 7's, and 8's. In addition, any number larger than 16 can be written by adding 5's to one of these five numbers.

So, the answer is 11.

18. A circle O has radius 8. Another circle P intersects O at A and B. If the arc AB measures 60 degrees with respect to O and 90 degrees with respect to P, then what is the square of the radius of P?

Answer (32):

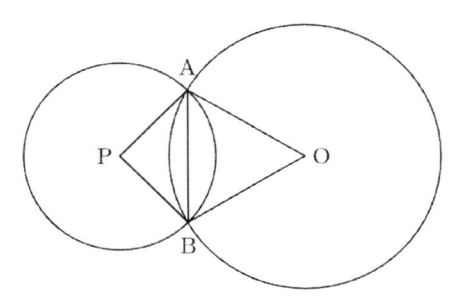

Since the arc $\overset{\frown}{AB}$ has measure 60 degrees, we know that triangle ABO is an equilateral triangle, so $AB = 8$. Since ABP is an isosceles right triangle with right angle at P, we find that
$$AP = BP = \frac{AB}{\sqrt{2}} = \frac{8}{\sqrt{2}} = 4\sqrt{2}.$$

Thus, the answer is $(4\sqrt{2})^2 = 32$.

19. Let a and b be distinct real numbers that satisfy
$$(5 + a - b)^2 - (5 - a + b)^2 = (4 + a + b)^2 - (4 - a - b)^2.$$

What is $\left(\frac{a}{b}\right)^2$?

Answer (81): Observe that for anuy numbers x and y, we have
$$(x + y)^2 - (x - y)^2 = 4xy.$$

Taking $x = 5$ and $y = a - b$, we have
$$(5 + a - b)^2 - (5 - a + b)^2 = 4 \cdot 5(a - b).$$

Taking $x = 4$ and $y = a + b$, we have

$$(4 + a + b)^2 - (4 - a - b)^2 = 4 \cdot 4(a + b).$$

Hence,

$$4 \cdot 5(a - b) = 4 \cdot 4(a + b).$$

Simplifying this, we get

$$a = 9b.$$

Thus, $\frac{a}{b} = 9$ and $\left(\frac{a}{b}\right)^2 = 81$.

Alternate Solution: Using the difference of squares factoring

$$x^2 - y^2 = (x - y)(x + y),$$

we get

$$\begin{aligned}
(5 + a - b)^2 - (5 - a + b)^2 &= (4 + a + b)^2 - (4 - a - b)^2 \\
(2a - 2b) \cdot 10 &= (2a + 2b) \cdot 8 \\
20a - 20b &= 16a + 16b \\
4a &= 36b \\
a &= 9b.
\end{aligned}$$

As before, we conclude that

$$\left(\frac{a}{b}\right)^2 = 9^2 = 81.$$

20. In chess, a bishop can attack a piece that is on the same diagonal as itself. A king can attack any piece that is in any one of the 8 adjacent spots as itself. If m is the maximum number of kings you can place on an 8×8 chessboard such that no king can attack each other, and n is the maximum number of bishops you can place on a different 8×8 chessboard such that no bishop can attack each other, what is $m + n$? The diagram below shows how the bishop and king attack on the chessboard, with B denoting the bishop and K denoting the king.

Test-3 Solutions

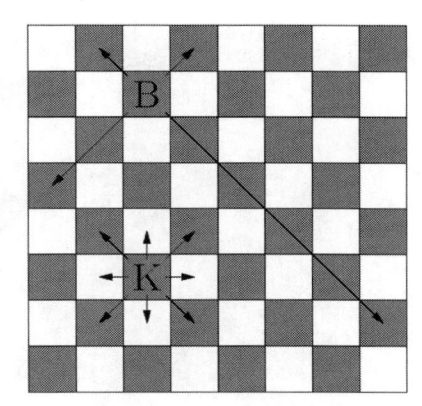

Answer (30): We claim that the maximum number of kings is $m = 16$. This can be achieved when we place a king on every column i and row j such that i and j are both odd, as shown in the diagram below.

We now show that we cannot place more than 16 kings. Split the squares on the chessboard into 16 regions, each region consisting of a 2×2 square. Each of these 2×2 squares can have at most 1 king in them, or else the two kings would attack each other. Since there are 16 of these regions, then we must have at most 16 kings that will not attack each other. We have already shown that 16 kings is possible above, so this is our desired maximum.

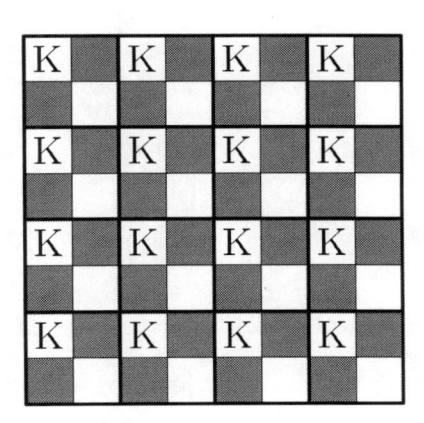

Now, we find n. Split the board into 15 diagonals going in the direction of northwest - southeast (this includes the one from the upper left to the bottom right), two of which are one-by-one squares. At most one bishop can go on each of these diagonals. However, on the two end diagonals (the two opposite corners), only 1 bishop can go on the two, since they share the same diagonal in the other direction. Thus, the maximum number of bishops is at most 14. This is achievable if you put 8 bishops on the top row, and 6 on the center 6 squares of the bottom row, as in the diagram shown below. So, $n = 14$.

Therefore, the answer is $m + n = 30$.

21. Let p, q, and r be primes satisfying

$$3p + q = r^2 - 30.$$

What is the sum of all possible values of $p + q + r$?

Answer (22): Note that if p, q, r were all odd, the equation would not be true, as $3p + q$ would be even but $r^2 - 30$ would be odd. So, at least one of these primes must be even, and hence equal to 2.

Since $r^2 - 30$ is positive, $r > 2$ and cannot be 2.

If $p = 2$, then
$$q = r^2 - 36 = r^2 - 6^2 = (r-6)(r+6).$$

As q is prime, one of the factors must be 1, so $r - 6 = 1$, which gives

$$(p, q, r) = (2, 13, 7).$$

If $q = 2$, then $3p + 32 = r^2$. This would imply that $r^2 = 3p + 22$ has remainder 2 when divided by 3. But squares can only have remainders of 0 or 1 when divided by 3. So, this case has no solution.

Hence, the answer is $2 + 13 + 7 = 22$.

22. In $\triangle ABC$, $AB = 8$ and $AC = 12$. If M is the midpoint of segment $\overline{AC}$ and $BM = 6$, then BC can be written in the form $m\sqrt{n}$, where n is not divisible by the square of any prime. What is the value of mn?

Answer (20):

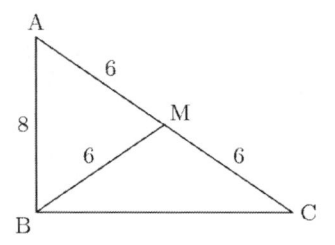

Since $BM = AM = CM = 6$, M must be the circumcenter of $\triangle ABC$. This means that AC is the diameter of the circumcircle of $\triangle ABC$, so $\overset{\frown}{AC} = 180$. By the Inscribed Angle Theorem, $\angle ABC = 90$. Thus, by Pythagorean Theorem,

$$BC^2 = AC^2 - AB^2 = 12^2 - 8^2 = 80$$
$$BC = 4\sqrt{5}.$$

So, the answer is $mn = 4 \cdot 5 = 20$.

Alternate Solution: Using that $\triangle AMB$ and $\triangle BMC$ are isosceles triangles, we get

$$\angle B = \angle ABM + \angle MBC = \angle A + \angle C.$$

Adding $\angle B$ to both sides we get

$$2\angle B = \angle A + \angle B + \angle C$$
$$2\angle B = 180°$$
$$\angle B = 90°.$$

Now, as before, using Pythagorean Theorem, we get $BC = 4\sqrt{5}$.

23. Let r, s, and t be the solutions of the equation

$$x^3 - 3x^2 - 6x + 2 = 0.$$

What is $r^3 + s^3 + t^3$?

Answer (75): We can rewrite the eqaution as
$$x^3 = 3x^2 + 6x - 2.$$

Adding this for $x = r, s,$ and t, we get
$$r^3 + s^3 + t^3 = 3(r^2 + s^2 + t^2) + 6(r + s + t) - 6.$$

By Vieta's Formulas, or by writing
$$x^3 - 3x^2 - 6x + 2 = (x - r)(x - s)(x - t),$$

then expanding and equating the coefficients for x^2 and x terms, we have
$$r + s + t = 3$$

and
$$rs + st + rt = -6.$$

Using these, we get
$$\begin{aligned} (r + s + t)^2 &= (r^2 + s^2 + t^2) + 2(rs + st + tr) \\ 3^2 &= r^2 + s^2 + t^2 + 2 \cdot (-6) \\ r^2 + s^2 + t^2 &= 21. \end{aligned}$$

Finally, substituting this back in the sum of cubes equation, we find
$$\begin{aligned} r^3 + s^3 + t^3 &= 3(r^2 + s^2 + t^2) + 6(r + s + t) - 6 \\ &= 3 \cdot 21 + 6 \cdot 3 - 6 \\ &= 75. \end{aligned}$$

24. A semicircle ω with center O has diameter $AB = 2$. A smaller semicircle ω_1 with center O_1 and passing through O is inscribed in ω. Another semicircle ω_2 whose center O_2 lies on $\overline{AB}$ is drawn such that it passes through A and it is externally tangent to ω_1. If the radius of ω_2 is $\frac{a-\sqrt{b}}{c}$, such that a, b, c are positive integers and b is not divisible by the square of any prime, what is $a + b + c$?

Test-3 Solutions 61

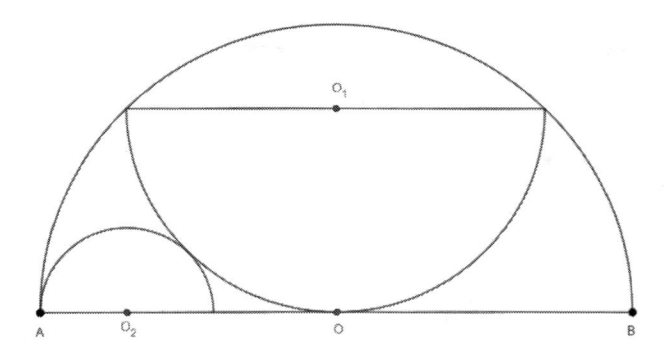

Answer (6):

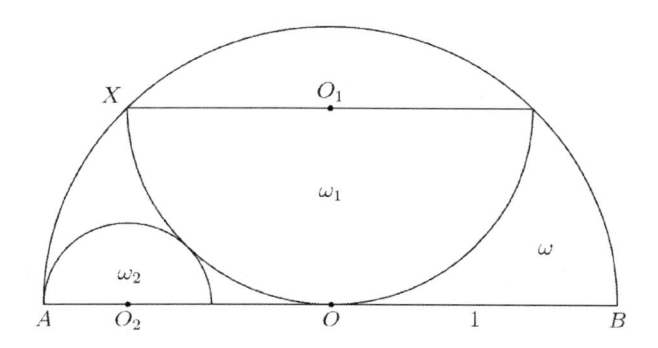

Let X be an intersection point of ω and ω_1, as shown in the diagram above. Then note that $\triangle XOO_1$ is a 45-45-90 triangle with hypotenuse $OX = OA = 1$. So, the radius of ω_1 is $\frac{\sqrt{2}}{2}$.

Let the radius of ω_2 be r. Then,

$$\overline{O_2O_1} = r + \frac{\sqrt{2}}{2}.$$

Also,

$$OO_2 = OA - O_2A = 1 - r.$$

Since $\triangle O_2OO_1$ is a right triangle, then by the Pythagorean Theorem,

$$(1-r)^2 + \left(\frac{\sqrt{2}}{2}\right)^2 = \left(r + \frac{\sqrt{2}}{2}\right)^2.$$

Solving this, we get

$$1 - 2r + r^2 + \frac{1}{2} = r^2 + \sqrt{2}r + \frac{1}{2}$$
$$(2 + \sqrt{2})r = 1$$
$$r = \frac{1}{2 + \sqrt{2}}$$
$$r = \frac{2 - \sqrt{2}}{2}.$$

So, the answer is $2 + 2 + 2 = 6$.

25. Two distinct numbers a and b are selected from $\{1, 2, 3, ..., 9\}$. What is the number of possible distinct values of $\text{lcm}(a, b)$?

   Answer (26): Let $N = \text{lcm}(a, b)$. We will do casework on the number of prime factors of N. We have
   $$1 \cdot 2 \leq N \leq a \cdot b \leq 8 \cdot 9 = 72.$$
   Since
   $$2 \leq N < 2 \cdot 3 \cdot 5 \cdot 7,$$
   the number of prime factors of N is at least one and at most three.

   One prime factor: This gives 7 possible N values:
   $$2, 2^2, 2^3, 3, 3^2, 5, \text{ and } 7.$$

   Two prime factors: We can pair up any 2 of the prime powers from case 1 (not of the same prime). 2 has three powers less than 10, 3 has two powers less than 10, 5 and 7 each have one power less than 10. Therefore, we have a total of
   $$3 \cdot (2 + 1 + 1) + 2 \cdot (1 + 1) + 1 \cdot 1 = 17$$
   possible N values in this case.

   Three prime factors: One of the 2 numbers must have 2 prime factors, and only 6 has this property. Thus, the only 2 values we can have are $(2 \cdot 3) \cdot 5$ and $(2 \cdot 3) \cdot 7$.

   In total, there are $7 + 17 + 2 = 26$ possible N values.

Pi Math Contest VOL 3

2019 Fermat Final Round

INSTRUCTIONS

1. This is a twenty-five-question test. Each question has an answer among the numbers 0, 1, 2, ..., 98, 99.

2. SCORING: You will receive 10 points for each correct answer, 1 point for each problem left unanswered, and 0 points for each incorrect answer.

3. No computational aids are permitted other than Ruler and Compass. No calculators are allowed. No problems on the test *require* the use of a calculator.

4. Figures are not necessarily drawn to scale.

5. You will have **40 minutes** to complete the test.

1. There are 5 blue balls and 15 red balls in a bag. What percent of the balls in the bag are blue?

2. How many ways are there to order the letters in the word CAT?

3. Simplify
$$\frac{9 - 0.01}{0.3 - 0.01}.$$

4. Compute $3^{4/6} \times 9^{2/3} \times 81^{1/2}$.

5. Find the side length of a cube whose volume is numerically equal to 6 times its surface area.

6. Find the sum of all integers a such that $\dfrac{a^2}{200}$ and $\dfrac{20}{a^2+1}$ are both less than 1.

7. A, B, and C are three distinct elements from the set $\left\{-8, -2, -\dfrac{1}{2}, \dfrac{1}{4}, 1, 4\right\}$. What is the largest possible value of $A \times B \div C$?

8. A rectangle with dimensions 32 and 72 is cut into 3 pieces and a square is formed by rearranging these pieces. Find the side length of the square.

9. How many four-digit palindromes are divisible by 6? A palindrome is a number that remains the same when its digits are reversed. For example: 343 is a palindrome.

10. Two circles share the same center. Both circles have integer radius. The area of the region inside the larger circle and outside the smaller circle is 707π. Find the smallest possible value of the radius of the larger circle.

11. How many perfect squares less than 10,000 are divisible by 6?

12. N is the product of two different primes. The positive difference between N and the sum of the positive divisors of N is 50. What is N?

13. An (infinite) increasing arithmetic sequence of integers starts with 1 and does not contain 101. How many such sequences are there whose second term is less than 100?

14. Find $ax + by + cz$ if

$$ax = by = cz,$$
$$\frac{1}{a} + \frac{1}{b} + \frac{1}{c} = 8,$$
$$x + y + z = 144.$$

15. How many ordered pairs (x, y) of positive integers satisfy the equation

$$6x + 15y = 2019?$$

16. $T^E = ABLE$ where T, A, B, L and E are distinct non-zero digits and $ABLE$ is a four-digit number. Find $T + A + B + L + E$.

17. In a chess tournament with 5 players, each player plays every other player twice. A player receives 3 points for a win, 1 point for a tie and no points for a loss. At the end of the tournament, Xavier has 20 points, Yoshiko has 18 points, Zoe has 12 points, Tally has 4 points, and Quentin has 2 points. How many games ended in a tie?

18. Ms. Turtle is going from her house to her office. One third of the distance between her house and her office is flat, one third is downhill and the rest is uphill. Her average speeds on flat roads, downhill roads, and uphill roads, are 60 mph, 90 mph, and 36 mph, respectively. What is her average speed (in mph) for the entire trip?

19. P, Q, R are three similar triangles with areas proportional to 1, 4, and 9, in some order. If P has perimeter 12, what is the sum of all possible perimeters of Q?

20. Today is May 4, 2019. Jolly the Jellyfish was born in November 1876 and is now 52019 days old. She observes that

$$52019 = 365 \times 142 + 189$$

and that since she was born, there have been 34 leap days. What day of the month was it when Jolly was born?

21. How many non-congruent triangles with integer side lengths have perimeter 15?

22. Lines l_1 and l_2 in the figure below are parallel. Suppose all possible line segments are drawn between A, B, C, D, E, F and G, H, I, J. At most how many intersections can exist in the interior region between l_1 and l_2? (Do not count intersections on l_1 or l_2!)

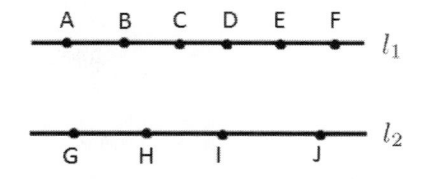

23. In triangle ABC, points M and N are on AB and AC respectively such that $BC = CM = MN = NA = 10$. CM is the interior angle bisector of the triangle ABC. Find the largest integer less than or equal to the length of BN.

24. $A_1, A_2, A_3, \ldots$ are sets of numbers satisfying the following properties:

    - A_i has i elements.
    - The average of the numbers in the set A_i is equal to i.
    - The intersection of any two sets is empty.

    We take the union of two different sets A_m and A_n and get the set B. The average of the numbers in B is 10. What is the sum of all possible values of $m + n$?

25. Evaluate
$$\frac{\left(\sqrt{54} + \sqrt{26} + \sqrt{8}\right)\left(\sqrt{54} + \sqrt{26} - \sqrt{8}\right)\left(\sqrt{54} - \sqrt{26} + \sqrt{8}\right)\left(-\sqrt{54} + \sqrt{26} + \sqrt{8}\right)}{16}.$$

Test-4 Answer Key

1. 25
2. 6
3. 31
4. 81
5. 36
6. 0
7. 64
8. 48
9. 13
10. 54
11. 17
12. 94
13. 90
14. 54
15. 67
16. 21
17. 4
18. 54
19. 96
20. 30
21. 7
22. 90
23. 17
24. 34
25. 27

Test-4 Solutions

1. There are 5 blue balls and 15 red balls in a bag. What percent of the balls in the bag are blue?

   Answer (25): There are 20 balls in the bag. 5/20 or 25 percent are blue.

2. How many ways are there to order the letters in the word CAT?

   Answer (6): There are 3 ways to choose the first letter, 2 ways to choose the second letter, and 1 way to choose the last letter. So the answer is $3 \times 2 \times 1 = \boxed{6}$. The six orderings are
   $$ACT, \ ATC, \ CAT, \ CTA, \ TAC, \ TCA.$$

3. Simplify
   $$\frac{9 - 0.01}{0.3 - 0.01}.$$

   Answer (31): Multiplying the numerator and the denominator by 100 we get
   $$\frac{900 - 1}{30 - 1} = \frac{30^2 - 1}{30 - 1} = \frac{(30 - 1) \times (30 + 1)}{30 - 1} = 30 + 1 = 31.$$

4. Compute $3^{4/6} \times 9^{2/3} \times 81^{1/2}$.

Answer (81):
$$3^{4/6} \times 9^{2/3} \times 81^{1/2} = 81^{1/6} \times 81^{1/3} \times 81^{1/2}$$
$$= 81^{\left(\frac{1}{6}+\frac{1}{3}+\frac{1}{2}\right)}$$
$$= 81.$$

5. Find the side length of a cube whose volume is numerically equal to 6 times its surface area.

   Answer (36): Let x be the side length of the cube. Our cube must satisfy:
   $$x^3 = 6 \times \left(6x^2\right).$$
   Since $x \neq 0$, we get $x = 36$.

6. Find the sum of all integers a such that $\dfrac{a^2}{200}$ and $\dfrac{20}{a^2+1}$ are both less than 1.

   Answer (0): Note that if an integer a satisfies the given conditions, then so does $-a$. Hence the sum of all such integers is $\boxed{0}$.

7. A, B, and C are three distinct elements from the set $\left\{-8, -2, -\dfrac{1}{2}, \dfrac{1}{4}, 1, 4\right\}$. What is the largest possible value of $A \times B \div C$?

   Answer (64): To be as large as possible, we need the expression to be positive, so we need either 0 or 2 of A, B, C to be negative. We also want $|A|$ and $|B|$ to be as large as possible and $|C|$ to be as small as possible. There are two viable candidates we should check:
   $$\frac{(-8) \times 4}{-1/2} = 64$$
   $$\frac{(-8) \times (-2)}{1/4} = 64$$
   Both lead to the same answer, and this is indeed the largest possible value: 64.

Test-4 Solutions

8. A rectangle with dimensions 32 and 72 is cut into 3 pieces and a square is formed by rearranging these pieces. Find the side length of the square.

   Answer (48): The total area of the rectangle is
   $$32 \times 72 = 64 \times 36 = 8^2 \times 6^2 = 48^2.$$
   This is also the area of the resulting square. Therefore, the side length of the square is 48.

9. How many four-digit palindromes are divisible by 6? A palindrome is a number that remains the same when its digits are reversed. For example: 343 is a palindrome.

   Answer (13): To be divisible by 6, the integer must be divisible by 2 and 3. Thus we are looking for even palindromes whose digits add up to a multiple of 3.

   The first and last digits must be same nonzero even digits: $2, 4, 6, 8$. The second and third digits must be so that the entire digit sum is divisible by 3. If the middle two digits are positive, we get 3 solutions for each of the four choices of the first digit, as shown below:
   $$2112, 2442, 2772$$
   $$4224, 4554, 4884$$
   $$6336, 6666, 6996$$
   $$8118, 8448, 8778$$
   This gives $4 \times 3 = 12$ solutions. Moreover, if the second and third digits are 0, 6006 also works. Therefore, the total number of valid palindromes is 13.

10. Two circles share the same center. Both circles have integer radius. The area of the region inside the larger circle and outside the smaller circle is 707π. Find the smallest possible value of the radius of the larger circle.

    Answer (54): Let r and R be radii of the smaller and larger circle, respectively. Then the area of the region inside the larger circle and outside the smaller circle is $R^2\pi - r^2\pi$. Hence $R^2 - r^2 = 707$. Then $(R-r)(R+r) = 707 = 7 \times 101$. Since r and R are integers and $R > r$, we either have $R - r = 1$ and $R + r = 707$ or we have $R - r = 7$ and $R + r = 101$. Solving for R, we get $R = 354$ or $R = 54$. The smallest possible value of R is 54.

11. How many perfect squares less than 10,000 are divisible by 6?

    Answer (17): If a perfect square is a multiple of 6, then it is a multiple of 2 and 3. Therefore, it must be the square of a number which is a multiple of 2 and 3 (or a multiple of 6).

    Since $\sqrt{10,000} = 100$, the number can be
    $$(6 \times 0)^2, (6 \times 1)^2, (6 \times 2)^2, \ldots, (6 \times 16)^2.$$
    Hence, the answer is $16 + 1 = 17$.

12. N is the product of two different primes. The positive difference between N and the sum of the positive divisors of N is 50. What is N?

    Answer (94): Let $N = pq$, where p and q are two primes with $p < q$. Then the positive divisors of N are $1, p, q,$ and pq. Hence $(1 + p + q + pq) - pq = 1 + p + q = 50$, which implies $p + q = 49$. As 49 is odd, we must have $p = 2$. So $q = 47$ and $N = pq = 94$.

13. An (infinite) increasing arithmetic sequence of integers starts with 1 and does not contain 101. How many such sequences are there whose second term is less than 100?

    Answer (90): The arithmetic sequence looks like:
    $$(1, 1 + d, 1 + 2d, 1 + 3d, \ldots)$$
    for some positive integer d. Since the second term of the sequence is less than 100, there are 98 choices for d: $1, 2, 3, \ldots, 98$.

    However, some of these lead to sequences that **do** contain 101. Consider such a sequence. Then there exists some positive integer k such that
    $$1 + kd = 101,$$
    or
    $$kd = 100.$$

Thus the number of such invalid sequences is the number of positive divisors of 100, excluding $k = 1$ (because we cannot have $d = 100$). Therefore, there are 8 possible values of k. Our final answer is
$$98 - 8 = 90.$$

14. Find $ax + by + cz$ if

$$ax = by = cz,$$
$$\frac{1}{a} + \frac{1}{b} + \frac{1}{c} = 8,$$
$$x + y + z = 144.$$

Answer (54): Let $G = ax = by = cz$. Then, $\frac{1}{a} = \frac{x}{G}$, $\frac{1}{b} = \frac{y}{G}$, and $\frac{1}{c} = \frac{z}{G}$. Hence,
$$8 = \frac{1}{a} + \frac{1}{b} + \frac{1}{c} = \frac{x+y+z}{G} = \frac{144}{G}.$$
Therefore, $G = 18$ and $ax + by + cz = 3G = 54$.

Alternatively, one can observe that letting $x = y = z$ and $a = b = c$ leads to the solution $x = y = z = 48$ and $a = b = c = \frac{3}{8}$. Hence, the answer is
$$3 \times 48 \times \frac{3}{8} = 54.$$

15. How many ordered pairs (x, y) of positive integers satisfy the equation
$$6x + 15y = 2019?$$

Answer (67): First, we divide the equation by 3 to yield $2x + 5y = 673$. Looking at the parity of both sides, we note that y must be odd. Since x is positive, $5y < 673$, so we find that the largest odd value y can attain is 133. Hence, $y = 1, 3, 5, \ldots, 133$ (with corresponding x values $334, 329, 324, \ldots, 4$). This yields $\frac{133+1}{2} = 67$ pairs of solutions.

16. $T^E = ABLE$ where T, A, B, L and E are distinct non-zero digits and $ABLE$ is a four-digit number. Find $T + A + B + L + E$.

Answer (21): Note that $2 \leq T \leq 9$, which means T^E is a power of 2, 3, 5, 6, or 7 (powers of 4 and 8 are already powers of 2; powers of 9 are already powers of 3). Looking for powers of these numbers that give a four-digit number with non-zero distinct digits, we get the following list

$$2^{13} = 8192, \quad 3^7 = 2187, \quad 5^5 = 3125, \quad 6^4 = 1296.$$

Among these, only $3^7 = 2187$ gives rise to a solution with

$$T + A + B + L + E = 3 + 2 + 1 + 8 + 7 = 21.$$

17. In a chess tournament with 5 players, each player plays every other player twice. A player receives 3 points for a win, 1 point for a tie and no points for a loss. At the end of the tournament, Xavier has 20 points, Yoshiko has 18 points, Zoe has 12 points, Tally has 4 points, and Quentin has 2 points. How many games ended in a tie?

Answer (4): There are $2 \times \binom{5}{2} = 20$ games. If no games were tied, $3 \times 20 = 60$ points would be distributed to the players. Every time a game ends in a tie, 1 fewer point is distributed ($1 + 1$ versus 3). Since the total number of points distributed is $20 + 18 + 12 + 4 + 2 = 56$, we conclude that $60 - 56 = \boxed{4}$ games must have ended in a tie.

Test-4 Solutions

18. Ms. Turtle is going from her house to her office. One third of the distance between her house and her office is flat, one third is downhill and the rest is uphill. Her average speeds on flat roads, downhill roads, and uphill roads, are 60 mph, 90 mph, and 36 mph, respectively. What is her average speed (in mph) for the entire trip?

    Answer (54): Let D be the distance of $\frac{1}{3}$ of the route in miles.
    Average speed for the journey is total distance traveled divided by total time. The total distance traveled is $3D$. To find total time, we add the times from each third of the route:
    $$\frac{D}{60} + \frac{D}{90} + \frac{D}{36} = \frac{D}{18}.$$
    Finally, the average speed for the entire journey is:
    $$\frac{3D}{\left(\frac{D}{18}\right)} = 54 \text{ mph}.$$

    Alternatively, note that the average speed does not depend on the distance. This is because if distance is scaled by a factor, total time is scaled by that same factor. So we may let the distance be something convenient for calculation purposes. Let the total distance be 540 miles. Then each third is 180 miles and the trip takes
    $$\frac{180}{60} + \frac{180}{90} + \frac{180}{36} = 3 + 2 + 5 = 10 \text{ hours}.$$
    The average speed then is $\frac{540}{10} = 54$ mph.

19. P, Q, R are three similar triangles with areas proportional to 1, 4, and 9, in some order. If P has perimeter 12, what is the sum of all possible perimeters of Q?

    Answer (96): If the areas are in the ratio of $1^2, 2^2, 3^2$, then the perimeters must be in the ratio of 1, 2, 3. Since P has perimeter 12, the sum of the possible values for the perimeter of Q is
    $$\begin{aligned} & 12 \times \left(\frac{1}{2} + \frac{1}{3} + \frac{2}{1} + \frac{2}{3} + \frac{3}{1} + \frac{3}{2}\right) \\ =\ & 6 + 4 + 24 + 8 + 36 + 18 \\ =\ & 96. \end{aligned}$$

20. Today is May 4, 2019. Jolly the Jellyfish was born in November 1876 and is now 52019 days old. She observes that

$$52019 = 365 \times 142 + 189$$

and that since she was born, there have been 34 leap days. What day of the month was it when Jolly was born?

Answer (30): Because there have been 34 leap days in the 142 years since Jolly was born, $365 \times 142 + 34$ days ago must also be same day of the year as today, a May 4th (of 1877). We need to go back another $189 - 34 = 155$ days. Going back $155 = 4 + 30 + 31 + 28 + 31 + 31$ days from May 4, we arrive at November 30. So the answer is 30. Note that in the last part we counted February as 28 days since the year 1877 is not a leap year.

21. How many non-congruent triangles with integer side lengths have perimeter 15?

Answer (7): Suppose the side lengths of the triangle are a, b, and c with $a+b+c = 15$. Without loss of generality, assume $a \leq b \leq c$. We can do casework on c, the longest side. By the triangle inequality, $c < a+b$. Adding c to both sides, we get $2c < a+b+c = 15$. Hence, c can be at most 7. Also, being the largest of the three, c must be at least the average, which is 5.

- **Case 1:** $c = 7$. Then $a + b = 8$; listing out the possibilities gives $(a, b, c) = (1, 7, 7), (2, 6, 7), (3, 5, 7), (4, 4, 7)$ or 4 triangles.
- **Case 2:** $c = 6$. Then $a + b = 9$; listing again gives $(3, 6, 6), (4, 5, 6)$ or 2 triangles.
- **Case 3:** $c = 5$. The only triangle is $(a, b, c) = (5, 5, 5)$.

Altogether there are $4 + 2 + 1 = \boxed{7}$ triangles.

22. Lines l_1 and l_2 in the figure below are parallel. Suppose all possible line segments are drawn between A, B, C, D, E, F and G, H, I, J. At most how many intersections can exist in the interior region between l_1 and l_2? (Do not count intersections on l_1 or l_2!)

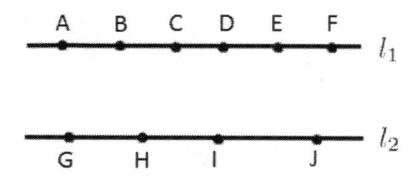

Answer (90): Note that every intersection point corresponds to the intersection of the diagonals of a unique trapezoid with two points on l_1 and two points on l_2. Conversely, every such trapezoid gives rise to a unique intersection point. So the number of intersection points is the same as the number of such trapezoids. There are $\binom{6}{2} = 15$ ways to choose the two points on l_1 and $\binom{4}{2} = 6$ ways to choose the two points on l_2. This gives us $15 \times 6 = 90$ trapezoids.

23. In triangle ABC, points M and N are on AB and AC respectively such that $BC = CM = MN = NA = 10$. CM is the interior angle bisector of the triangle ABC. Find the largest integer less than or equal to the length of BN.

    Answer (17): Let $\angle BAC = \theta$. Doing some angle chasing using isosceles triangles $\triangle MNA$, $\triangle NMC$, $\triangle BCM$, we find that $\angle NMA = \theta$, $\angle CNM = \angle NCM = \angle MCB = 2\theta$, $\angle CBM = \angle CMB = 3\theta$.

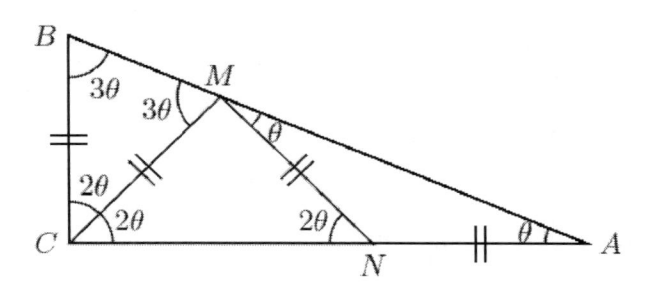

    The sum of the angles in $\triangle BCM$ is $8\theta = 180°$, so $2\theta = 45°$. We then see that $\triangle CMN$ is a right isosceles triangle. Hence, $CN = 10\sqrt{2}$. Moreover, $\triangle BCA$ is a right triangle and using Pythaorean Theorem one more time on $\triangle BCN$ with legs 10 and $10\sqrt{2}$ we get $BN = 10\sqrt{3}$, which is between 17 and 18. Hence the answer is 17.

24. $A_1, A_2, A_3, \ldots$ are sets of numbers satisfying the following properties:

    - A_i has i elements.
    - The average of the numbers in the set A_i is equal to i.
    - The intersection of any two sets is empty.

We take the union of two different sets A_m and A_n and get the set B. The average of the numbers in B is 10. What is the sum of all possible values of $m + n$?

Answer (34): Without loss of generality, assume that $m < n$. We need to find the sum of the elements of B, which has $m + n$ elements. The sum of the elements of A_m is m^2 since there are m elements in A_m and their average is m. Likewise, the sum of the elements of A_n is n^2. So $m^2 + n^2$ is the sum of the elements of B. The average of the numbers in B, 10, is given by:

$$10 = \frac{m^2 + n^2}{m + n}$$

for some positive integers m and n. It will help us to rewrite this as:

$$m^2 + n^2 - 10m - 10n = 0.$$

We want to "complete the square." That is:

$$(m^2 - 10m + 25) + (n^2 - 10n + 25) = 50,$$
$$(m - 5)^2 + (n - 5)^2 = 50.$$

We are looking for two perfect squares which add up to 50. The only possibilities are $25 + 25$ and $1 + 49$.
$25 + 25$ case leads to the candidates $(m, n) = (5 \pm 5, 5 \pm 5)$ none of which is a solution (remember that we need $0 < m < n$).
$1 + 49$ case leads to the candidates

$$(m, n) = (5 \pm 1, 5 \pm 7), (5 \pm 7, 5 \pm 1).$$

Among these, only $(4, 12)$ and $(6, 12)$ work. Hence, $m + n$ can be 16 or 18 and the answer is 34.

25. Evaluate

$$\frac{\left(\sqrt{54} + \sqrt{26} + \sqrt{8}\right)\left(\sqrt{54} + \sqrt{26} - \sqrt{8}\right)\left(\sqrt{54} - \sqrt{26} + \sqrt{8}\right)\left(-\sqrt{54} + \sqrt{26} + \sqrt{8}\right)}{16}.$$

Answer (27): We repeatedly use difference of squares. We start with multiplying the first two terms in the numerator:

$$\begin{aligned}\left(\sqrt{54} + \sqrt{26} + \sqrt{8}\right)\left(\sqrt{54} + \sqrt{26} - \sqrt{8}\right) &= \left(\sqrt{54} + \sqrt{26}\right)^2 - \left(\sqrt{8}\right)^2 \\ &= (80 + 2\sqrt{54} \times \sqrt{26}) - 8 \\ &= 72 + 12\sqrt{39}.\end{aligned}$$

Test-4 Solutions

Next we multiply the last two terms in the numerator:

$$\left(\sqrt{54}-\sqrt{26}+\sqrt{8}\right)\left(-\sqrt{54}+\sqrt{26}+\sqrt{8}\right) = \left(\sqrt{8}\right)^2 - \left(\sqrt{54}-\sqrt{26}\right)^2$$
$$= 8 - (80 - 2\sqrt{54} \times \sqrt{26})$$
$$= 12\sqrt{39} - 72.$$

Finally, we combine these two

$$(12\sqrt{39}+72)(12\sqrt{39}-72) = (12\sqrt{39})^2 - 72^2$$
$$12^2(39-6^2) = 12^2 \times 3 = 4^2 \times 3^3 = 16 \times 27.$$

Alternative Solution: One can notice that the given expression (via Heron's Formula) is the square of the area of the triangle with side lengths $\sqrt{54}$, $\sqrt{26}$, and $\sqrt{8}$. We can find the area of this triangle by reconstructing it using two right triangles: $\sqrt{2} - \sqrt{6} - \sqrt{8}$ and $\sqrt{2} - \sqrt{24} - \sqrt{26}$.

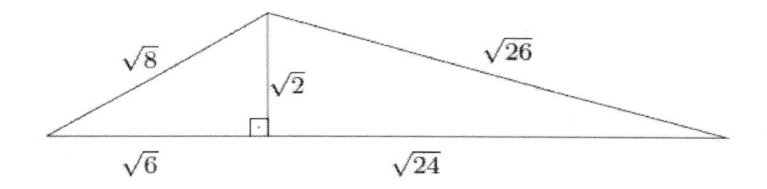

The area is then

$$\frac{(\sqrt{6}+\sqrt{24}) \times \sqrt{2}}{2} = 3\sqrt{3}.$$

Hence, the answer is $(3\sqrt{3})^2 = 27$.

Made in the USA
Las Vegas, NV
14 March 2024

87209937R00050